TABLE OF CONTENTS

Foreword 4

Glossary 5

Introduction 7

- Aquariums and Their Underlying Philosophies 7
- Days of Creation 7
- The Fall 7
- Death 8
- The Flood 8
- Extinction 8
- Animal Kinds and Adaptations 9
- Defense/Attack Structures 9
- Evolution 10
- Natural Selection 10
- Ocean Zones 10
- Symbiosis 11
- Marine Mammals 12

Stewardship 13

The Good News 13

* Bony Fish 15

* Cartilaginous Fish 89

* Invertebrates 113

* Birds 171

* Mammals 195

* Reptiles 211

** Note: Throughout this aquarium guide, animals are listed alphabetically. However, the animals in these sections have been grouped together for easy access since most aquariums have grouped many, if not all, of these animals in the same location. The animals within these sections are also listed alphabetically.*

FOREWORD

Few places intrigue the mind and fascinate the imagination like the public aquarium. Because of the vast variety of sea creatures in the world's oceans and seas today, no two aquariums are alike in what animals they display. However, all too often aquariums teach the evolutionary message of millions of years and common ancestry. As we take our children or students to the aquarium, we must be prepared to confront this evolutionary teaching with the truths of the Bible. We should be equipped with a biblical understanding of God's Word. This *Aquarium Guide* is designed to equip you and your children or students with the biblical knowledge necessary to counter the evolutionary message of these aquariums.

The introductory pages of the *Aquarium Guide* provide foundational information to help you better understand the beginning of our world and the effects of the Fall of man on all of creation. They also give you a biblical perspective on such topics as evolution, natural selection, animal kinds, the uniqueness of marine mammals, symbiotic relationships, and extinction. Each animal information page includes the animal's scientific classification, size, habitat and range, features, fun facts, and design elements. These pages direct our attention to the Creator God and His creativity and handiwork in His creation.

This *Aquarium Guide* provides all ages with Bible-based information that refutes the evolutionary interpretation you see at the aquarium. The animals we see at the aquarium are amazing testaments to God's handiwork. The *Aquarium Guide* provides the correct perspective on these marvelous creatures.

GLOSSARY

Atoll A circular coral island not associated with an existing coastal area

Bivalve A mollusk that has a shell consisting of two hinged valves, including clams, oysters, and mussels

Carapace The hard outer covering or case of certain organisms such as arthropods; in turtles, their dorsal (top) shell only is the carapace

Carrion Dead and decaying flesh

Cephalopod Any mollusk of the class Cephalopoda having tentacles attached to the head, including the cuttlefish, squid, and octopus

Chromatophore A pigment-containing or pigment-producing cell that by expansion or contraction can change the color of the skin of some animals, such as the squid or octopus

Cilia Minute hairlike organelles on the surface of some cells, identical in structure to flagella

Crest A showy tuft of feathers on a bird's head

Crustacean A class of arthropods having a hard shell, segmented body, and jointed appendages, including lobsters, crabs, crayfish, shrimp, and barnacles

Diurnal Occurring or active during the daytime rather than at night

Echolocation A process of using sound waves and their reflection to locate objects

Ecosystem An community of organisms together with its environment, functioning as a unit

Estuarine Of, relating to, or found in an estuary

Estuary The wide part of a river near the sea where fresh and salt water mix

Exoskeleton A hard outer structure that provides protection or support for an organism, such as the shell of an insect

Fin(s)
- **Anal fin** The fin on the bottom side of the fish near the fish's tail
- **Caudal fin** The tail fin, which provides the main power for forward movement in fish
- **Dorsal fin** The fin on the "top" of the fish
- **Pectoral fins** Pair of fins on each side of the fish, near the head, behind the gill openings
- **Pelvic fins** Pair of fins attached to the pelvic girdle in fishes that help control the direction of movement

Flight feathers Feathers specifically designed to enable a bird to fly

Gastropod Any mollusk of the class Gastropoda having a head with eyes and feelers and a muscular foot on the underside of its body, such as a snail, slug, or limpet

Gills The fleshy organs that most aquatic animals use to extract oxygen from water

Habitat The area or environment where an organism or ecological community normally lives

Hibernation Cessation from or slowing of activity during the winter involving a slowing of metabolism

Ichthyology That branch of zoology dealing with fishes

Indo-Pacific Pertaining to the areas of the Indian and Pacific oceans off the coast of SE Asia

Invertebrate	A creature that does not have a backbone
Kind	The original organisms created supernaturally by God as described in Genesis 1 (and their descendants) that reproduce only with members of their own kind within the limits of pre-programmed information, but with great variation
Mammal	Any of various warm-blooded, vertebrate animals characterized by a covering of hair on the skin and, in the female, milk-producing mammary glands for nourishing the young
Mantle	A fold or pair of folds of the body wall that lines the shell and secretes the substance that forms the shell in mollusks and brachiopods
Marine	Native to or inhabiting the sea
Mollusk	An invertebrate of the phylum Mollusca that has a soft unsegmented body, a mantle, and a protective shell (with the exception of nudibranchs)
Mutualism	A relationship between two species that benefits both species
Naturalism	The system of thought holding that all phenomena can be explained in terms of natural causes and laws without recourse to spiritual or supernatural explanations
Nocturnal	Occurring or active during the night rather than in daytime
Nudibranch	Marine gastropod that lacks a shell and gills but has finger-like projections that serve as respiratory organs; also called sea slug
Oviparous	A method of animal reproduction in which eggs are laid by the female and develop outside the body
Ovoviviparous	A method of animal reproduction in which fertilized eggs develop within the female and the embryo gains no nutritional sustenance from the female
Plankton	Tiny plant (phytoplankton) and animal (zooplankton) organisms floating in seas and lakes
Radula	A flexible tongue-like organ in certain mollusks, having rows of horny teeth on the surface
Rudimentary	Imperfectly or incompletely developed
School	A group of fish
Scute	An external bony plate or a large modified scale, as in the shell of a turtle
Spawning	The release of eggs by female fish in the water and their fertilization by males
Spicule	Small pointed structure serving as a skeletal element in various marine and freshwater invertebrates such as sponges and corals
Spinule	A small spine
Substratum	A surface on which an organism grows or is attached
Symbiosis	A close interaction between creatures of two different species
Venomous	Having a gland or glands for secreting venom; able to inflict a poisoned bite, sting, or wound
Vertebrate	A creature that has a backbone
Viviparous	A method of reproduction in which the embryo develops inside the body of the female from which it gains nourishment

INTRODUCTION

Aquariums and Their Underlying Philosophies

Excitement and anticipation always accompany trips to the aquarium. And why not? Aquariums are filled with unusual and fascinating creatures that many people have never seen before. The aquarium is a place where children can watch and learn from the animal kingdom up close and personal. But what lessons are aquariums teaching? Are they teaching the true history of each creature? In most cases, if not all, aquariums teach evolution and naturalism—teachings that are not in God's Word. On exhibit plaques and brochures throughout aquariums, the teachings of evolution claim that every feature of every animal is the result of natural processes that occurred by chance. As you take your trip through the aquarium, enjoy the wonders of God's creation, but be aware of the teaching that is set before your eyes and minds and the eyes and minds of your children or students. Aquariums have their own philosophies about the origins of life, and those philosophies will be displayed throughout the aquarium. Look for those philosophies, and use them to teach your children and to remind yourselves of God's hand in nature.

Days of Creation

In Genesis 1, God tells us how and when He created everything. The Bible tells us that on Day 1 God created the earth, space, time, and light. On Day 2 He separated the waters on and above the earth. On Day 3 He created dry land and all the plants. On Day 4 God created the sun, moon, and stars; and on Day 5 He created the sea animals and all flying creatures. On Day 6 God created the land animals and man. When God created the first man and woman, He made them different from the animals. He created Adam out of the dust of the ground and Eve out of Adam's rib. God created man and woman in His image so that they could have a relationship with their Creator God. Now, the animals that we see in the aquarium probably do not look exactly like the animal kinds that God originally created on Day 5; but we will discuss that later (see Animal Kinds and Adaptations on page 9). According to the Bible, God took six days close to 6,000 years ago to create all the original kinds of plants and animals, the whole universe—the sun, moon, and stars—and Adam and Eve. Everything was perfect, and God called all He had created "very good."

The Fall

God's creation was perfect; there was no sickness, pain, or death. But this perfect creation did not last long. God placed Adam and Eve in the Garden of Eden where they could enjoy all of His creation. God gave Adam and Eve a rule: Don't eat of the Tree of the Knowledge of Good and Evil. God told them that if they ate of it, they would die. One day Eve was walking in the Garden, and the serpent spoke to her. He questioned God's goodness to Eve, and he tempted her to eat the fruit from the Tree of the Knowledge of Good and Evil. Eve ate of the fruit and disobeyed God. She then gave the fruit to Adam, and he ate. This disobedience was sin against a holy God. And since God is completely holy, He had to punish sin. God had warned Adam and Eve that if they ate of the Tree, they would die. When God came to walk with them that evening, He punished their sin. The earth was now cursed.

Death was now part of life; both animals and humans would now die (Genesis 3:19; Romans 8:20–22). When the first humans sinned, it changed all of creation. The ground was cursed and would produce weeds and thorns (Genesis 3:17–18). Animals began to hunt other animals. Man would now have to work hard for food, and woman would have pain in bearing and raising her children. All mankind would now be born with a sin nature, which causes us to reject God. Adam and Eve's first sin is what we call the Fall.

Death

Since death was a result of the Fall, you may wonder what Adam, Eve, and the animals ate when they were first created. The answer is simple. According to God's Word, they ate plants (Genesis 1:29–30). Even though this answer sounds simple, it has caused some to wonder about the difference between plant life, animal life, and human life. The Bible says that death was a result of the Fall (Romans 5:12), but if plants died before the Fall, then death was present before sin. The difference between plant life, animal life, and human life is spoken of in the Word of God. Throughout the Bible, the Hebrew word *nephesh chayyâh* is used to describe human and animal life. When referring to mankind, *nephesh chayyâh* is often translated as "living soul." When referring to animals, it is translated "living creature." However, this word is never applied to plant life. There is a plain distinction. It is easy to see that plants do not experience pain, suffering, or death in the same way that humans and animals do. Their death is not the death of a "living soul" or "living creature." Therefore, the eating of plants did not constitute death before the Fall. Possibly included with plants are the simpler invertebrates, since they too were excluded from the *nephesh chayyâh* creatures. Therefore, some animals may have originally also eaten insects and other simpler invertebrates. To gain a better understanding that there was no "living creature death" before the Fall of Adam, we must interpret the Bible correctly and read what God has written. God's Word plainly teaches that death is the result of sin. Therefore, there was no human or animal (*nephesh chayyâh*) death before sin. Adam, Eve, and all the animals ate plants before the Fall.

The Flood

Ever since Adam, man has continued to turn his back on his Creator and has done his own thing. The people grew so wicked that God decided to destroy the earth and everything that lived on the earth. But God knew one man who followed Him. That man was Noah. God spoke with Noah and told Noah that He was going to destroy all the earth by water—a global flood. However, God wished to spare Noah. He told Noah to build an Ark, which would preserve his wife, his sons, their wives, and two of every kind of air-breathing, land animal and bird (and seven of some). This boat was huge, measuring over 400 ft (122 m) long and 75 ft (23 m) wide and 45 ft (13.5 m) tall. It took Noah quite a while to build his boat; but once he, his family, and the animals were on board, God closed the door. Then for 40 days and nights, the water in the atmosphere fell and the waters in the earth came out. For 150 days water covered the whole earth, covering even the earth's highest hills by over 22 ft (7 m). And the waters remained on the earth for over a year, until Noah and his family could leave the Ark. All the people and land animals outside the Ark died. The force of the waters was so powerful that tons of soil and sediment were moved around during the Flood. Plants, animals, and even humans were buried in this sediment. Some of these bones have been dug up today; they are called fossils. Not all fossils are from the Flood, but most of them are. After the floodwaters drained into the ocean basins, the whole earth was changed—mountains, valleys, the climate ... everything.

Extinction

When all members of a certain species of animal dies out, it is said to be extinct. Extinction may occur because of changes in habitat, disease, starvation, or by hunting. Many animals have become extinct in the past, and extinction can happen to any animal. One extinct animal (as far as we know) that everyone is fascinated by is the dinosaur. When talking about the dinosaurs, or any other extinct animal, we must keep some things in mind. First, we know that dinosaurs were real because their bones have been discovered and preserved for us to see. The Bible says that land animals were created on Day 6, and, since dinosaurs were land animals, they were included in this creation. Second, we must remember that when God sent the Flood to punish mankind's wickedness, He preserved His creation by sending animals onto the Ark. Dinosaurs would have also been on the Ark and preserved from the Flood. Dinosaurs could have fit on the Ark, since they were on average about the size of a small pony; and God most likely would have sent young dinosaurs to Noah since they were to repopulate the world after the Flood. Third, since representatives of the dinosaur kinds were on the Ark and survived the Flood, something must have happened to them after that, which caused them to die out. There are many things that could have contributed to the extinction of the dinosaurs, including climate change, starvation, diseases, and hunting by humans and/or other animals (some of the same reasons animals today become extinct!). Finally, we should remember that some animals that were thought to have been extinct for a long time have actually been found alive and well in different parts of the world (for example, the coelacanth). So, is it possible to ever find a live dinosaur on earth again? Maybe.

Animal Kinds and Adaptations

On Days 5 and 6 God created the various animal kinds. What is an animal kind? A kind represents a group of animals that came from the same created ancestor; most likely animals that can cross-breed with each other today are from the same created kind. Kind is not necessarily the same grouping as the species that we use today. For example, lions, tigers, jaguars, and leopards are classified as different species, but are probably all members of an original cat kind. And donkeys, zebras, and thoroughbred and Arabian horses are probably all part of the original horse kind. What did this original kind look like? We don't know for sure, but the representatives of each kind had enough information in their DNA to produce the wide variety of animals that we see today. (DNA is the molecule inside the body's cells that contains the genetic information that will determine the growth and development of that organism.) For more information on the original kinds, see www.answersingenesis.org/liger.

Defense/Attack Structures

The Bible tells us that before the Fall, every animal ate only plants (Genesis 1:29–30). Death (including animal death) entered the world as a result of Adam's sin (Romans 5:12; 8:20–22). It was only after the Flood that God gave man permission to eat other things besides plants (Genesis 9:3). As you look at the animals in the aquarium, you may wonder how there could be no animal death before Adam sinned, when so many animals look like they were designed to attack and eat other animals or to defend themselves from other animals. There are several possible explanations.

First, the harmful structures (like sharp teeth, poison, and claws) may have been used for different functions before the Fall, and animals only began to use them for attack and defense afterward.

A second possibility is that the defense or attack structures may have changed into what they are today by mutations or other processes.

A third option is that the animals may have been redesigned after the Fall as part of God's curse on all of creation, including the animals (remember, the form of the serpent was changed—Genesis 3:14).

And finally, it is also possible that since God foreknew the Fall would happen, the information for these structures could have been "programmed" in the first animals, and that the information was "switched on" after the Fall. The most important thing to remember about defense and attack structures is that they were not part of God's original creation; they came about as a result of the Curse on creation after Adam sinned.

Evolution

A popular belief today is that all animals and humans evolved (changed) from one kind into another kind over millions of years. Evolution claims that everything we see happened by purely natural processes. Some believe that in the beginning God created simple lifeforms and then let natural processes take over, so that what we see today evolved from these early, simple lifeforms. Some say that there is no God who created or began anything. These people would say that everything is the result of time and natural processes, that everything happened by accident. Evolution often includes the belief that life formed from something that was not living, and then that life evolved over millions of years into the different animals we have today. Most evolutionists even believe that humans evolved from ape-like creatures and that dinosaurs evolved into birds. Scientists have demonstrated for us that these things are just not possible: life can't come from non-living chemicals; animals don't change into other kinds of animals. Even though evolution is taught in most public and private school textbooks, molecules-to-man evolution, where one kind changes into a completely new kind has never been observed. This concept is based on the ideas of man, not on the Bible, which comes from God.

Natural Selection

Many evolutionists claim that natural selection is the process that drives evolution. However, natural selection actually works in the opposite direction of what molecules-to-man evolution requires. Evolution requires that, over time, living things must add more information to their DNA as they gain new features, abilities, or structures. However, scientists have shown us that this doesn't happen. But scientists have observed that animals reproduce "after their kind," just as the Bible teaches (dogs have puppies, cats have kittens, geese have goslings, kangaroos have joeys, etc.). Sometimes, some animals aren't born with the ability to survive in their environment. Natural selection is the process by which animals die out when they don't have the ability to adapt to their surroundings. Those animals that have the ability to adapt are able to survive and reproduce more animals like themselves. For example, many animals that live in drier regions of the world are able to gain most of the water they need from the plants they eat. Animals without this ability would have a harder time trying to survive in that region and would eventually die out. God created the original animal kinds with much diversity in their DNA, so that as they reproduced and filled the earth, their descendants would be able to adapt to many different environments. Natural selection may bring about a new species within a kind, but it cannot generate a new kind of animal.

Ocean Zones

Water covers nearly 71% of the earth's surface. Freshwater rivers and lakes, as well as saltwater seas and open oceans, are part of this aquatic ecosystem. Lakes, ponds, and oceans are divided into zones based on water depth and distance from the shore.

Lakes and Ponds

Lakes and ponds are divided into the photic and aphotic zones. The photic zone is made up of the shallow water close to the shore and the upper zone of water away from the shore. The aphotic zone is found in the deep areas of a pond or lake. The photic zone is so named because light can penetrate its depths. The aphotic zone is the depth at which light cannot penetrate. The bottom of lakes and ponds is included as a separate zone, called the benthic zone. This zone is made up of rock, sand, and other sediments.

Oceans

Ocean zones that signify the distance from the shore include the intertidal zone, neritic zone, and oceanic zone. The two zones of depth are called the benthic zone, which is the seafloor, and the pelagic zone, which is the ocean's open water.

Intertidal

The intertidal zone is the area of shore that is exposed to the sun during low tide and covered by water during high tide. This zone can be sandy or rocky.

Neritic

The neritic zone is the area from the low tide line to the edge of the continental shelf. Most coral reefs and aquatic life inhabit the neritic zone. For the most part, sunlight reaches the bottom of the neritic zone, which extends to a depth of about 656 ft (200 m).

Oceanic

The oceanic zone occurs from the edge of the continental shelf outward. It is also subdivided into the photic and aphotic zones, similar to lakes and ponds. However, some scientists have subdivided the oceanic zone into the epipelagic zone, the mesopelagic zone, the bathypelagic zone, the abyssopelagic zone, and the hadalpelagic zone. These five zones are divided mainly by their depth. The epipelagic zone extends from the ocean's surface down to 656 ft (200 m); the mesopelagic zone extends from 656 ft to 3,280 ft (1,000 m). The bathypelagic zone extends from 3,280 ft to 13,124 ft (4,000 m), and the abyssopelagic zone extends from 13,124 ft to 19,686 ft (6,000 m). The hadalpelagic zone extends from 19,686 ft to 32,810 ft (10,000 m). This zone consists of the areas in the deep water trenches and canyons.

Symbiosis

Have you ever been to the dentist? Did you know that fish go to the "dentist" and to the "doctor"? It's true. Many fish, especially after eating a meal, will go to a nearby cleaning station and wait in line for specialized cleaners to clean their mouths. While the larger fish may prey on smaller fish and shrimp throughout the day to stay alive, they will hold their mouths open while the cleaner picks them clean of food debris and parasites. They will even open their gills so that the cleaner can remove parasites from those areas. Whales and other large sea creatures are also hosts to smaller cleaners that remove harmful parasites from their skin. This type of relationship between two different animals is called symbiosis, and when it benefits both creatures—the cleaner eats the food debris and parasites, and the "cleanee" gets cleansed of things that could harm it—it is called mutualism. Such a relationship does not logically follow the evolutionary mentality of survival of the fittest, where each creature struggles against every other creature to survive. Instead, mutualistic relationships are an example of the amazing way the Creator provides and cares for His creation.

Marine Mammals

Marine mammals, mammals that live in the water, are equipped with some unique design features that can only be the result of an all-knowing Creator.

Underwater birth

Air-breathing land mammals are normally born headfirst; but air-breathing marine mammals would be in serious danger if they too were born headfirst. Instead, marine mammals, like whales and dolphins, give birth to their young tailfirst. Some "breach" births do occur (born headfirst), but this is not the norm. Since the baby is born in water, it is critical that the baby does not take its first breath until it reaches the water's surface. Being born tailfirst allows the head and nostrils (blowhole on whales and dolphins) to emerge last. The baby then is pushed up or swims instinctively to the water's surface to breathe. This design prevents a newborn from inhaling water and drowning, even though this does happen sometimes.

Streamlined bodies

Like all true mammals, marine mammals have some hair. Whales, dolphins, and porpoises are born with a few "bristles" of hair, usually around the head or mouth. Most will lose these bristles after a few days. The fur of marine mammals like sea lions, walruses, and seals lies flat against their bodies while they are swimming. This allows these animals to swim through the water with very little resistance. The limbs of marine mammals are also designed as flippers or paddles that act as "wings" to propel them through the water. The tail flukes of whales, dolphins, and manatees move up and down (not side-to-side like fish). This arches the animal's back, bringing its head (blowhole or nostrils) up so the animal can breathe while swimming.

Echolocation

This amazing design feature allows whales and dolphins to hear while underwater. Normally, we think that the blowhole is only used to let the whale or dolphin breathe. However the blowhole is also used in echolocation, which aids these sea creatures in finding food and in maneuvering through the water. The blowhole is not connected to the throat, as some people think. When the whale or dolphin is underwater it closes the flap of its blowhole (or blowholes depending on the species), so that water does not enter. There are many air passageways under the blowhole that eventually connect to the lungs. When the whale inhales, air is trapped in these passages. With the airways sealed off, the whale can force the air from one passageway to another while restricting the opening of the passageway. When the whale does this, it does not lose air; it simply recycles it from one passage to another passage. The sound that results from this air being forced through a restricted passage is the squeaking we often hear whales and dolphins make. These sounds are actually vibrations that are sent out from the passageways.

The vibrations travel out the front of the forehead through the "melon," a large blob of fatty tissue located in the forehead in front of the animal's blowhole. The shape of the melon can be reconfigured to act as a "lens" to focus the sound vibrations out in front of the creature's head. These focused vibrations travel out away from the animal and continue until they strike an object. The vibrations then return to the head of the creature in the form of an echo, which is picked up by the bones in its jaw and skull. These vibrations are processed immediately and translated into meaningful data for the animal. The animal can tell what the object is, if it is moving, and possibly even the density of the object.

These amazing features are not the result of chance, random processes of evolutionary change from a land-dwelling mammal to a sea-dwelling mammal. These features are the result of the careful design of these creatures' Creator God who designed them to survive and thrive in their watery habitat.

Stewardship

After God created Adam and Eve, He told them to be fruitful and multiply and to have dominion over the creation (Genesis 1:26–28). They were to tend the Garden and to eat from its produce. They were also to care for the animals. God owns the earth (Psalm 24:1), but He has asked us to be responsible stewards of His creation (which is now suffering from the Curse). We can do this by not littering or polluting our air or water unnecessarily. Stewardship can be taken to an extreme of placing the animals over humans, but we need to be careful to avoid this mentality. Man is God's special creation, since we were created in His image (Genesis 1:26–27). Let's all do our part in being good stewards of the world that God gave us so that others can also enjoy it in the years to come.

The Good News

When Adam sinned, all of creation was cursed. Part of that curse on man was separation between God and man. Before the Fall, Adam and Eve had walked with God in perfect fellowship, but after the Fall, sin separated man from his Creator. And sin continues to separate us from God. God is perfect and requires those who come to live with Him to also be perfect. But since we are born with a sin nature and because we sin against God daily, we can never get to heaven by anything that we do. And since God must punish sin as He punished Adam and Eve's sin in the Garden, our punishment is an eternity separated from God. It sounds hopeless, unless there is someone who would be willing to pay our sin penalty for us. That someone must be without sin—perfect. Jesus, the Son of God, is that perfect God-man who took upon Himself the penalty for our sin. Jesus died on a cross, paying for our sin; and three days later He rose again, defeating death to provide us with a way to one day live with Him. But for us to be acceptable to God, we must repent of our sins and place our faith in Jesus. We must believe that Jesus took our place on the Cross and died for us. Even though some people say that there are many ways to God, there is actually only one way. Jesus said in John 14:6, "I am the way, the truth, and the life. No one comes to the Father except through Me." Jesus is the only way to be reconciled with God. We can never earn eternal life on our own because of our sin. Jesus paid our penalty and made a way for us to live with Him forever. We must repent of our sin and place our trust in Him—that is the good news.

ARCHERFISH

ARCHERFISH

CREATED ON DAY 5

DESIGN

The archerfish gets its name from its ability to shoot a precisely-aimed stream of water at its prey, which are mostly insects living on land. The archerfish's special ability relies heavily on its vision. It has been shown that the archerfish can see its victim through the water without the image being distorted. The information for this ability was given to the archerfish by its Creator; it did not slowly evolve this ability over millions of years.

FEATURES

- Archerfish can vary in color, but most of them have either silver or yellow bodies with vertical black bars.

FUN FACTS

- The archerfish can shoot an insect up to 6 ft (1.8 m) above the water's surface.
- This fish also jumps out of the water to catch its prey in mid-air.
- The archerfish automatically adjusts the force it uses to dislodge its prey according to the size of its prey.

CLASS: Actinopterygii (ray-finned fishes)
ORDER: Perciformes (perch-like fishes)
FAMILY: Toxotidae (archerfishes)
GENUS/SPECIES: *Toxotes* (Seven different species)

Size: Average 10 in (25.4 cm); up to 16 in (40 cm)
Depth: Shallow waters
Habitat: Swamps of India, New Guinea, Australia, the Philippines, and Southeast Asia

AUSTRALIAN LUNGFISH

AUSTRALIAN LUNGFISH

CREATED ON DAY 5

DESIGN

The fossils of a creature almost identical to the Australian lungfish were found in Northern Ireland and were dated at 100 million years. With the Australian lungfish being limited to the waters of Queensland, Australia, how did remains of this creature get in Northern Ireland? Simple. Before the global Flood, the Australian lungfish may not have been limited to its present region. Also, the effects of the Flood could have moved this creature to the area of present-day Northern Ireland and buried it for people to find later. These fossil finds are an amazing testimony to God's hand in creating the lungfish kind and to His hand in covering the entire earth in a global Flood.

FEATURES

- The Australian lungfish has a long, heavy body that is covered with large, overlapping scales.
- Its coloring is brown to green. Some have dark spots near the tail.
- The adult's belly is white, but the young's belly can be an orange-pink.
- Its fins are stiff and resemble flippers instead of fins.

FUN FACTS

- This creature is also known as the Queensland lungfish.
- During periods of drought, this fish can survive by breathing air, surfacing one or two times each hour, when the supply of oxygen in the water is low.
- Of all the lungfish species, the Australian lungfish is the only one that has a single lung.
- The oldest known Australian lungfish is 80 years old or older.

CLASS:	Sarcopterygii (lobe-finned fishes and terrestrial vertebrates)
ORDER:	Lepidosireniformes (lungfishes)
FAMILY:	Ceratodontidae (lungfishes)
GENUS/SPECIES:	*Neoceratodus forsteri*
Size:	Up to 4.5 ft (1.4 m); commonly 3 ft (1 m)
Diet:	Frogs, fish, shrimp, earthworms, plants, and fallen fruit
Habitat:	In the deep pools of slow-flowing waters of Queensland, Australia

BARRACUDA

BARRACUDA

CREATED ON DAY 5

DESIGN

The barracuda was created with keen eyesight. It uses this design feature to effectively hunt its prey. Originally, this creature did not eat meat; it ate plants since all animals were created vegetarians.

FEATURES

- The barracuda is very muscular and is shaped like a torpedo.
- It has dozens of sharp teeth that line its jaws.

FUN FACTS

- Some of the barracuda's teeth point backward into its mouth to help prevent fish from slipping out.
- The barracuda likes shiny objects; it thinks such objects are food. When diving in an area where barracudas may be found, don't wear jewelry or other shiny objects. The barracuda may think you are food.
- A large barracuda is capable of cutting a large parrotfish in two with a single bite.

CLASS:	Actinopterygii (ray-finned fishes)
ORDER:	Perciformes (perch-like fishes)
FAMILY:	Sphyraenidae (barracudas)
GENUS/SPECIES:	18 species
Size:	Varies depending on species, 1.5–10 ft (0.5–3 m)
Diet:	Almost any fish
Habitat:	All temperate and tropical waters, except the eastern Pacific and the Mediterranean Sea

BUTTERFLYFISH

BUTTERFLYFISH

CREATED ON DAY 5

DESIGN

The butterflyfish is a laterally thin fish. This shape allows it to maneuver through the coral reef with relative ease. It also allows it to chase its prey into the coral. This design, given to the creature's original created kind by its Creator, shows His care.

FEATURES

- Butterflyfish are named for their brightly-colored and patterned bodies, which can be shades of red, blue, white, black, orange, and yellow.
- Many species exhibit dark eyespots on their sides and dark bands across their eyes.

FUN FACTS

- The largest butterflyfish species grows up to 11.8 in (30 cm).
- The color of a butterflyfish looks different at night than it does during the day.
- They are some of the most conspicuous of the coral reef fishes.
- The butterflyfish is typically diurnal.
- Most species occur as male/female pairs that may stay together for several years, or even for life.

CLASS:	Actinopterygii (ray-finned fishes)
ORDER:	Perciformes (perch-like fishes)
FAMILY:	Chaetodontidae (butterflyfishes)
GENUS/SPECIES:	127 species in 11 genera
Size:	4.7–8.5 in (12–21.5 cm)
Depth:	Mostly less than 60 ft (18 m); some species up to 590 ft (180 m)
Diet:	Coral polyps, crustaceans, and algae
Habitat:	Coral reefs of the oceans

CATFISH

CATFISH

CREATED ON DAY 5

DESIGN

Many species of this fish can adapt extremely well to their environment. They can endure temperatures of 45–95°F (8–35°C), and can live in waters that are poorly oxygenated. The catfish can also secrete mucus that keeps it from drying out if it finds itself in an evaporating body of water. These abilities to adapt to its changing habitat show the creativity of this creature's Creator.

FEATURES

- The catfish is named for its prominent barbels, or "whiskers," which look like cat's whiskers.
- The catfish has no scales, but has either thick leathery skin or armor.

FUN FACTS

- The North African catfish uses its pectoral fins and spines to crawl through shallow waters and across land.
- The catfish possesses strong, hollow, bony spines on the front of its dorsal and pectoral fins, through which a stinging protein can be delivered if the fish is irritated.
- The tiny Candiru catfish of the Amazon River will enter the body of a swimmer and begin to feed on blood and body tissue, sometimes causing death.

CLASS:	Actinopterygii (ray-finned fishes)
ORDER:	Siluriformes (catfishes)
FAMILY:	35 families
GENUS/SPECIES:	About 3,000 species
Size:	Varies widely; from 6 in (15 cm) to 10 ft (3 m)
Weight:	Varies widely; up to 600 lbs (270 kg)
Habitat:	Freshwaters throughout the world

CLEANER FISH

CLEANER FISH

CREATED ON DAY 5

DESIGN

This fish is called a cleaner fish because it attracts larger fish to its cleaning station where the larger fish are cleaned. The cleaner fish enters the other fish's mouth and gill openings to remove parasites and diseased tissue. This important role is uniquely given to this animal by its Creator to supply it with food, as well as other fish with a "doctor." Another feature to ensure the survival of the cleaner fish is the ability for a female fish to change into a male.

FEATURES

- The smooth, elongated body of the cleaner fish has very small scales that are brilliant blue with a band of black that runs from the snout to the tail.
- This fish has a small mouth with protruding lips and teeth.

FUN FACTS

- This fish is more commonly known as the blue streak wrasse.
- The cleaner fish will actually go to sleep at night. It retires to a small hole in the reef and sometimes covers itself with mucus.
- Although some cleaners do poorly in captivity, this species does well, learning to take a variety of standard aquarium foods.

CLASS: Actinopterygii (ray-finned fishes)
ORDER: Perciformes (perch-like fishes)
FAMILY: Labridae (wrasses)
GENUS/SPECIES: *Labroides dimidiatus*

Size: 4 in (10 cm)
Habitat: Indo-Pacific coral reefs, from Queensland and the South Seas to the Red Sea

CLOWN TRIGGERFISH

CLOWN TRIGGERFISH

CREATED ON DAY 5

DESIGN

The jaws of the clown triggerfish are extremely powerful. They can break open the shells of mollusks and crabs, which they eat. This characteristic is not the result of chance, random processes of evolution; it is the result of design by this creature's Creator.

FEATURES

- The clown triggerfish gets its name because of its unusual coloring and pattern.
- The lower half of this fish's body is black with large, white spots, and the upper half is mostly black with a patch outlined in yellow.
- The clown triggerfish's lips are bright orange.

FUN FACTS

- This fish is also called the big-spotted triggerfish.
- When alarmed or at night, the triggerfish wedges itself in a small hole by erecting its first dorsal spine. Fishermen discovered they could easily remove this fish from its hole by pressing on the second dorsal spine, which unlocks the first spine.
- The clown triggerfish is considered a highly prized aquarium fish, but it has a nasty disposition and usually requires a tank of its own.

CLASS:	Actinopterygii (ray-finned fishes)
ORDER:	Tetraodontiformes (cowfishes, filefishes, leatherjackets, puffers, triggerfishes, and trunkfishes)
FAMILY:	Balistidae (triggerfishes)
GENUS/SPECIES:	*Balistoides conspicillum*
Size:	Up to 20 in (50 cm)
Depth:	3–250 ft (1–75 m)
Diet:	Sea urchins, mollusks, and crustaceans
Habitat:	Tropical waters of the Pacific Ocean

COPPER ROCKFISH

COPPER ROCKFISH

CREATED ON DAY 5

DESIGN

The copper rockfish is viviparous—the female gives live birth rather than laying eggs, and it may nourish the larvae in the ovary. Unlike the salmon, which dies soon after spawning, the copper rockfish can live to reproduce year after year. Certainly, the Creator has designed this creature to reproduce abundantly.

FEATURES

- The color of this creature varies, but the most common color is brownish.
- Its fins are darker, and patches of yellow or copper are sometimes seen near its gill coverings.
- The copper rockfish also has a whitish underside.
- This fish can live to be more than 50 years old.

FUN FACTS

- At one time, this species was thought to be two separate species: *Sebastes caurinus* and *S. vexillaris*.
- The copper rockfish is sometimes called a chucklehead.
- The meat of this fish is tasty, firm, and flaky. It is excellent for fish and chips.

CLASS:	Actinopterygii (ray-finned fishes)
ORDER:	Scorpaeniformes (scorpion fishes and sculpins)
FAMILY:	Scorpaenidae (firefishes, goblinfishes, rockfishes, and scorpionfishes)
GENUS/SPECIES:	*Sebastes caurinus*
Size:	Up to 22 in (56 cm)
Weight:	Up to 6 lbs (2.7 kg)
Diet:	Crustaceans, squid, octopuses, smaller fish
Habitat:	Prefer the bottoms of the Pacific coast, from Baja, California up to Alaska; common near British Columbia and the Puget Sound

DISCUS FISH

DISCUS FISH

CREATED ON DAY 5

DESIGN

As with other cichlids, both discus fish parents care for the young. An amazing behavior of the discus fish, however, is just how it cares for the larvae. The adult discus produces a secretion through its skin, on which the larvae live during their first few days. The young can be seen "grazing" off their parents.

FEATURES

- The discus fish has a very flattened body shape. It is compressed from the sides into a discus shape, from where it gets its name.
- The sides of this fish are frequently patterned in shades of green, red, brown, and blue. The colors are patterned in vertical bars or horizontal stripes overlaid with wavy lines that extend into the dorsal and anal fins.

FUN FACTS

- The discus fish is native to the Amazon River basin.
- It is also a popular aquarium fish and has been called the king of the aquarium fishes.
- The colors of the discus fish will flare and become more distinct if the animal is startled or feels threatened.

CLASS:	Actinopterygii (ray-finned fishes)
ORDER:	Perciformes (perch-like fishes)
FAMILY:	Cichlidae (cichlids)
GENUS/SPECIES:	*Symphosodon aequifasciatus* (blue discus) and *Symphosodon discus* (red discus)
Size:	Up to 10 in (25 cm)
Diet:	Worms, crustaceans, insects, plant matter
Habitat:	Amazon River basin from Peru east to its mouth near Belem in Brazil

FRENCH ANGELFISH

FRENCH ANGELFISH

CREATED ON DAY 5

DESIGN

A young French angelfish has a unique "job" to perform in the ocean. It eats parasites that are using a number of other fish as hosts. For this reason the French angelfish is not attacked or harmed while performing this service. This symbiotic relationship gives evidence of the provision given to these sea creatures by their Creator.

FEATURES

- A young French angelfish is dark brown to black with yellow bands that curve across the head and body.
- The adult is black with yellow on the pectoral fin and around the eyes. Its face is light blue with white around the chin and mouth.
- The French angelfish is distinguished from the butterflyfish by the spine on its gill cover.

FUN FACTS

- The French angelfish changes color as it ages. When it is young, it is black with five vertical yellow bars; but as it ages, it loses the bars. Its black scales develop yellow edges.
- Each male defends a territory containing 2–5 females. He performs courtship displays and nuzzles the female at times.

CLASS:	Actinopterygii (ray-finned fishes)
ORDER:	Perciformes (perch-like fishes)
FAMILY:	Pomacanthidae (angelfishes)
GENUS/SPECIES:	*Pomacanthus paru*
Size:	Average 10–14 in (25–36 cm)
Depth:	10–330 ft (3–100 m)
Diet:	Sponges, algae, brine shrimp, and squid
Habitat:	Coral reefs in the Atlantic Ocean

GUPPY

GUPPY

CREATED ON DAY 5

DESIGN

The colors of different populations vary greatly depending on the number of predators. The fewer predators, the more colorful the guppy is. The more predators, the less colorful the guppy is. This feature is an adaptation of the guppy that occurred after the Fall.

FEATURES

- The female is brown in color, while the male may be almost any color with a colorful tailfin.

FUN FACTS

- The guppy is named after Robert John Lechmere Guppy of Trinidad, a naturalist and an early collector of the fish.
- The color of the guppy varies based on environmental conditions and the number of predators.
- This fish gives birth to live young; it does not lay eggs.
- The female guppy may give birth to between 20 and 100 young.

CLASS:	Actinopterygii (ray-finned fishes)
ORDER:	Cyprinodontiformes (killifishes)
FAMILY:	Poeciliidae (livebearers and topminnows)
GENUS/SPECIES:	*Poecilia reticulata*
Size:	Up to 1.5 in (4 cm); females are larger than males
Diet:	Algae, mosquito larvae, crustaceans, insects
Habitat:	Waters of Barbados, Trinidad, Central and South America

HUMPHEAD WRASSE

HUMPHEAD WRASSE

CREATED ON DAY 5

DESIGN

The humphead wrasse has large, plump lips that make this fish the perfect creature to control the growth of toxic and spiny reef creatures. The lips seem to absorb the spines of its prey so that the fish can chew its victim without hurting itself.

FEATURES

- The humphead wrasse is most recognized by a large hump on its head right above its eyes. This hump becomes more prominent with age.
- Males are blue or green, but females are shades of red, brown, or gray.
- It is among the largest of the reef fishes.

FUN FACTS

- This fish is also known as the Napoleon wrasse or Napoleonfish.
- It often has a "home" cave or crevice where it sleeps or enters when pursued.
- The humphead wrasse can change sex from female to male.

CLASS:	Actinopterygii (ray-finned fishes)
ORDER:	Perciformes (perch-like fishes)
FAMILY:	Labridae (wrasses)
GENUS/SPECIES:	*Cheilinus undulatus*
Size:	Up to 7.5 ft (2.3 m)
Diet:	Fish, mollusks, and sea urchins
Habitat:	Tropical waters of the Pacific Ocean, the Indian Ocean, and the Red Sea

LIONFISH

LIONFISH

CREATED ON DAY 5

DESIGN

Since the lionfish is a slow swimmer, it must be an efficient hunter. Its bold colors seen during the day actually act as camouflage during the early evening, which is the best time for hunting. The coloring blends the lionfish into its reef home, thus disguising it from its prey. The lionfish attacks in one swift motion. These attack capabilities were not active in God's original creation, since all animals were created as vegetarians.

FEATURES

- This unique creature has bright red or golden brown bands across its body.
- It also has long, feather-like pectoral fins and darkly spotted dorsal fins.

FUN FACTS

- The lionfish is equipped with up to 18 poisonous spines along its dorsal fin.
- This fish will often spread its feathery pectoral fins and herd smaller fish into a confined space where it can more easily swallow them.
- The lionfish is sometimes called the turkey fish, dragon fish, or scorpion fish.
- It is capable of inflicting extremely painful, and in some cases fatal, wounds.

CLASS:	Osteichthyes (bony fishes)
ORDER:	Scorpaeniformes (scorpionfishes and sculpins)
FAMILY:	Scorpaenidae (firefishes, goblinfishes, rockfishes, and scorpionfishes)
GENUS/SPECIES:	About 22 species in 5 genera
Size:	Up to 15 in (38 cm)
Weight:	Up to 2.6 lbs (1.2 kg)
Diet:	Small fish and crustaceans
Habitat:	Reefs of the Indo-Pacific region

LONGHORN COWFISH

LONGHORN COWFISH

CREATED ON DAY 5

DESIGN

When foraging, the longhorn cowfish often blows jets of water out of its mouth at the sand surface to uncover buried prey (this is known as hydraulic jetting). This is an effective method for uncovering hidden prey in sandy lagoon areas that the cowfish frequents.

FEATURES

- This fish is easily recognized by the two long horns that protrude from the front of its head, like those of a cow or bull, and the two spines that project backward at the rear of its body.
- The longhorn cowfish has a yellowish body with white or blue spots. Its horns and tail fin grow very long compared to its body size.
- The cowfish does not have an internal skeleton or scales, but rather a rigid, hard carapace from which the horns, fins, eyes, and lips protrude. This hard, shell-like body acts as protection against predators.

FUN FACTS

- This fish is also called the horned boxfish.
- The eyes of the cowfish move independently, so it is able to look in two different directions at the same time.
- The skin of the longhorn cowfish is poisonous, and when threatened it will release a toxin.

CLASS:	Actinopterygii (ray-finned fishes)
ORDER:	Tetraodontiformes (triggerfishes, pufferfishes, and spikefishes)
FAMILY:	Ostraciidae (boxfishes, cowfishes, and trunkfishes)
GENUS/SPECIES:	*Lactoria cornuta*
Size:	Up to 20 in (51 cm)
Depth:	Up to 165 ft (50 m)
Diet:	Algae and crustaceans
Habitat:	Sandy lagoons and coral reefs in the tropical waters of the Indo-Pacific region

LONGNOSE HAWKFISH

LONGNOSE HAWKFISH

CREATED ON DAY 5

DESIGN

The longnose hawkfish often makes its home among flame corals, which have stinging cells called nematocysts. Why doesn't the hawkfish get stung? The hawkfish has been designed with "skinless" pectoral fins, which allow it to come in contact with the stinging cells without getting stung.

FEATURES

- The longnose hawkfish is colored in a red and white netted design. It has a long needle-nosed snout which it uses to pull food from tight places.
- This fish has large pectoral fins, which are perfect for perching on rocks and coral.
- The hawkfish has cirri, or hair-like filaments, on the spines of its dorsal fin.

FUN FACTS

- The longnose hawkfish finds areas of coral, such as gorgonians (sea fans) and black corals, where it can perch and wait for food to swim or float by.
- This fish is perfectly camouflaged among the red gorgonians because of its matching tone and color.
- It often inhabits steep outer reef slopes exposed to strong currents.

CLASS:	Actinopterygii (ray-finned fishes)
ORDER:	Perciformes (perch-like fishes)
FAMILY:	Cirrhitidae (hawkfishes)
GENUS/SPECIES:	*Oxycirrhites typus*
Size:	Up to 5 in (13 cm)
Depth:	30–300 ft (10–100 m)
Diet:	Bottom-dwelling invertebrates and zooplankton
Habitat:	Indo-Pacific: Red Sea and South Africa to the Hawaiian Islands, north to southern Japan, south to New Caledonia; Eastern Pacific: Gulf of California to northern Colombia and the Galapagos Islands

LONG-SPINE PORCUPINEFISH

LONG-SPINE PORCUPINEFISH

CREATED ON DAY 5

DESIGN

The unique features of this fish give it protection against predators. When threatened, the long-spine porcupinefish will fill its body with air or water, which makes its body swell like a balloon. This makes it too large to fit into the predator's mouth. Also when "inflated," the spines all over its body are fully extended, making it even less of a desirable meal to the predator. Such a defense mechanism requires a flexible stomach, vertebrae, and sides. This structure could not have happened by chance, random processes, but was designed by the Creator.

FEATURES

- The long-spine porcupinefish has dark patches on its sides and back.
- It has long spines that protrude from all over its body, except for the fins and face.
- When not threatened, this fish's spines will lie flat against its body.

FUN FACTS

- Common names for this fish include balloonfish, balloon porcupinefish, blotched porcupinefish, brown porcupinefish, freckled porcupinefish, hedgehog fish, and spiny puffer.
- The long-spine porcupinefish has an elastic stomach, flexible skeletal structure, and stretchy skin, all which allow it to inflate like a balloon.
- The teeth of both the upper and lower jaws of this fish are fused, forming a solid, heavy beak. This beak makes cracking the shells of snails, sea urchins, and hermit crabs easy.

CLASS:	Actinopterygii (ray-finned fishes)
ORDER:	Tetraodontiformes (cowfishes, filefishes, leatherjackets, puffers, triggerfishes, and trunkfishes)
FAMILY:	Diodontidae (burrfishes and porcupinefishes)
GENUS/SPECIES:	*Diodon holocanthus*
Size:	Up to 24 in (60 cm)
Diet:	Mollusks, crabs, and sea urchins
Habitat:	Shallow areas in tropical waters of the world

LOOKDOWN

LOOKDOWN

CREATED ON DAY 5

DESIGN

The juvenile lookdown sports long filaments from its dorsal fin, which help it blend in with grasses. Light is reflected by guanine pigments in the lookdown's skin so that it flashes like a silver mirror.

FEATURES

- The lookdown is a shimmery, silvery fish with an extremely blunt forehead.
- Its body is also extremely compressed.

FUN FACTS

- This fish gets its name from the way it appears to look down its nose, like a snobbish person.
- This fish is sometimes known as the threadfin lookdown. Another name for the lookdown is the bluntnose. This name comes from its unusual shape.
- The lookdown is a summer and fall visitor to inshore areas from Maine to the Carolinas, as it prefers waters over 60°F (15°C).

CLASS:	Actinopterygii (ray-finned fishes)
ORDER:	Perciformes (perch-like fishes)
FAMILY:	Carangidae (jacks and pompanos)
GENUS/SPECIES:	*Selene vomer*
Size:	Average 6–10 in (15–25.4 cm)
Depth:	3–174 ft (1–53 m)
Diet:	Smaller fish, shrimp, squid, and small crabs
Habitat:	Coastal and estuarine waters of western Atlantic

MANDARINFISH

MANDARINFISH

CREATED ON DAY 5

DESIGN

The mandarinfish produces a thick mucous that covers its body. This mucous smells bad and tastes bitter. Scientists believe that this secretion could ward off potential predators. The bright colors of this fish could also give warning of its toxicity. These features may not have served this purpose until after the Fall of man since before the Fall all animals were vegetarian.

FEATURES

- The mandaranfish is distinguished by its bright colors and unusual shape.
- Its body is primarily blue with orange, red, and yellow wavy lines.

FUN FACTS

- The mandarinfish does not have scales; instead it produces a stinky mucous that covers its body.
- This fish is also called the mandarin dragonet.
- Mating between mandarinfish involves a ritualized dance.
- This is a very popular aquarium fish exported from the Philippines.

CLASS:	Actinopterygii (ray-finned fishes)
ORDER:	Perciformes (perch-like fishes)
FAMILY:	Callionymidae (dragonets)
GENUS/SPECIES:	*Synchiropus splendidus*
Size:	Up to 2.4 in (6 cm)
Depth:	Found at depths up to 60 ft (18 m)
Habitat:	Western Pacific tropical waters of the Philippines, Indonesia, Hong Kong, Australia, New Guinea, and the Ryukyu Islands in coral reefs and shallow lagoons

MOORISH IDOL

MOORISH IDOL

CREATED ON DAY 5

DESIGN

The bars of color on the body of the Moorish idol may serve as "disruptive coloration" that breaks up the body outline and makes it harder for predators to tell where the fish begins and ends. Some researchers suggest that the long, white dorsal fin may also serve to increase the fish's apparent size, so that it looks larger to potential predators.

FEATURES

- The Moorish idol has a compressed, disc-like body that has contrasting bands of black, white, and yellow.
- This fish has relatively small fins, except for the dorsal fin whose 6 or 7 spines are elongated to form a trailing, sickle-shaped crest.
- It has a tubular snout with a small mouth containing numerous bristle-like teeth.

FUN FACTS

- It is said the Moorish idol got its name from the Moors of Africa, who supposedly believed the fish to be a bringer of happiness.
- The Moorish idol is sometimes confused with the angelfish and the butterflyfish.
- This species is the only one in this fish family.

CLASS:	Actinopterygii (ray-finned fishes)
ORDER:	Perciformes (perch-like fishes)
FAMILY:	Zanclidae (Moorish idol)
GENUS/SPECIES:	*Zanclus cornutus*
Size:	Up to 9 in (23 cm)
Depth:	1–600 ft (3–180 m)
Diet:	Sponges and algae
Habitat:	The Indo-Pacific and tropical eastern Pacific, from East Africa to the Pacific coasts of the tropical Americas

MORAY EEL

MORAY EEL

CREATED ON DAY 5

DESIGN

The shape of the moray eel allows it to hunt prey that is larger than it can swallow. When the eel captures a large prey, it will wrap itself around the victim in a sort of knot and either flatten the prey's body enough to swallow it, or tear off a piece of its prey to eat it. This predatory behavior was not part of this creature's original design since all animals were created as vegetarians. They did not hunt other animals until after the Fall of man.

FEATURES

- The moray eel has a long, slender body with one long dorsal fin that runs along most of the back to the caudal fin (the tail) and into the anal fin, which runs along the underside of the body. Most species lack pectoral and pelvic fins.
- A moray has sharp, thin teeth that protrude from its upper and lower jaws, and sometimes from the roof of its mouth. Its teeth point backward to prevent slippery prey from escaping.

FUN FACTS

- The moray eel gets its color from the protective mucus it secretes that covers its body. This mucus contains a toxin in some species.
- The moray has a small, circular gill on each side of its head, well behind the mouth. The mouth is kept open (and moving) to help water circulate through the gills.
- This fish has poor eyesight but a very good sense of smell.
- Morays are edible and are hunted for food throughout much of the world.

CLASS:	Osteichthyes (bony fishes)
ORDER:	Anguilliformes (eels)
FAMILY:	Muraenidae (moray eels and morays)
GENUS/SPECIES:	200 species in 15 genera

Size:	From 6 in (15 cm) to 15 ft (4.5 m)
Weight:	Average 30 lbs (13.5 kg)
Diet:	Mostly fish, also crustaceans and octopuses
Habitat:	In rock crevices and small caves in all tropical seas and some temperate oceans

ORANGE CLOWNFISH

ORANGE CLOWNFISH

CREATED ON DAY 5

DESIGN

The relationship that the clownfish has with a sea anemone is truly a wonderful design feature. Very early in life, the clownfish must find a host with which to live. The sea anemone with its stinging tentacles is the perfect place for the easily preyed upon clownfish. However, the clownfish must develop a mucous that covers its body to protect it from the stings of the sea anemone. This mucous develops quickly after the clownfish brushes against the sea anemone. Once the mucous is completely formed, the clownfish is no longer prone to the effects of the sea anemone's tentacles. The sea anemone gives protection to the clownfish, and the clownfish helps feed, oxygenate, and remove waste materials from the sea anemone. This relationship shows God's creative hand in His creation.

FEATURES

- This species is easily identified by its bright orange body and three white, vertical bars.
- Each fin is outlined with black.

FUN FACTS

- The orange clownfish is also called the clown anemonefish, percula clownfish, true clownfish, and blackfinned clownfish.
- This fish eats the sea anemone's leftovers.
- Usually a female clownfish lives with other males in a group. When the female dies the head male changes sex and becomes the female.

CLASS:	Actinopterygii (ray-finned fishes)
ORDER:	Perciformes (perch-like fishes)
FAMILY:	Pomacentridae (damselfishes)
GENUS/SPECIES:	*Amphiprion percula*
Size:	2–5 in (5–13 cm)
Diet:	Algae, plankton, fish leftovers
Habitat:	Tropical waters of the Indo-Pacific region from Northern Queensland, Australia to Melanesia, including New Britain, New Guinea, New Ireland, the Solomon Islands, and Vanuatu

PARROTFISH

PARROTFISH

CREATED ON DAY 5

DESIGN

The teeth of the parrotfish are uniquely designed to scrape algae from coral and rocks. This is its main food source. Its Creator gave it an unusual "beak" to help it survive. It is also able to grind up pieces of coral and excrete the indigestible sand. These unique features were likely part of the original parrotfish kind when they were created on Day 5 of Creation Week.

FEATURES

- Species vary in size from the 5 inch Bluelip Parrotfish to the 4 foot Rainbow Parrotfish.
- Coloring ranges from reds to greens, blues and yellows, as well as grays, browns, and blacks.
- The parrotfish swims by rowing itself along with its pectoral (side) fins.

FUN FACTS

- This family was named "parrotfishes" because the shape of the teeth resembles a bird's beak, plus the fact that they are often brilliantly colored.
- Some species of parrotfish secrete a mucous envelope to sleep in. This mucous is thought to give it some protection form predators.
- In some species, if the dominant male in a harem should die, the dominant female fish will turn into a male to take his place.
- The parrotfish plays an important role in the health of the coral reef—it feeds on algae that could smother the coral if left to grow.

CLASS:	Actinopterygii (ray-finned fishes)
ORDER:	Perciformes (perch-like fishes)
FAMILY:	Scaridae (parrotfishes)
GENUS/SPECIES:	90 species in 10 genera
Size:	5 in–4 ft (0.13–1.2 m)
Diet:	Algae
Habitat:	Tropical coral reefs of the Caribbean, from the West Indies to Florida

PURPLE FIREFISH

PURPLE FIREFISH

CREATED ON DAY 5

DESIGN

The firefish's elongated dorsal fin is used to communicate with other firefish. It is also used to lodge itself into small cracks and crevices of a reef. This defense mechanism became part of the firefish's instincts only after the Fall since before the Fall all animals were vegetarian.

FEATURES

- The torpedo-like body of the purple firefish is colored light pink near its head and deepens into a deep red or orange at its tail.
- The upper lobes of the tail are almost black.
- It has an elongated dorsal fin.

FUN FACTS

- The purple firefish is aggressively territorial against other firefishes.
- It is sometimes called a dartfish because of its quick swimming style.
- Several firefishes, particularly juveniles, may utilize the same hole.

CLASS:	Actinopterygii (ray-finned fishes)
ORDER:	Perciformes (perch-like fishes)
FAMILY:	Microdesmidae (dartfishes and wormfishes)
GENUS/SPECIES:	*Nemateleotris decora*
Size:	Up to 3 in (7.6 cm)
Depth:	20–200 ft (6–60 m)
Diet:	Zooplankton and small crustaceans
Habitat:	Indo-Pacific region

RED-BELLIED PIRANHA

RED-BELLIED PIRANHA

CREATED ON DAY 5

DESIGN

These creatures hunt in packs of 20–30. They will either hide in vegetation and ambush prey, or they will chase after their prey. This hunting technique became part of the fish's instinct after the Fall.

FEATURES

- The coloring of this fish changes as it grows.
- Typically, this piranha is reddish-orange along its belly and silver along the top of its body.
- It has broad, serrated, razor-sharp teeth.

FUN FACTS

- The red-bellied piranha places its eggs in a nest.
- The danger of this piranha to humans is highly exaggerated since it hardly ever attacks humans.
- Tooth loss and replacement on alternating sides of the jaw allow the piranha to continue eating.

CLASS:	Osteichthyes (bony fishes)
ORDER:	Characiformes (leporins and piranhas)
FAMILY:	Characidae (American characins, characins, and tetras)
GENUS/SPECIES:	*Pygocentrus nattereri*
Size:	Up to 18 in (45 cm)
Diet:	Insects, worms, fish, and plants
Habitat:	Whitewater rivers of South America

REEF STONEFISH

REEF STONEFISH

CREATED ON DAY 5

DESIGN

This creature's amazing camouflage and attack structures point to its intelligent Creator. The original created kind did not need such defense/attack structures until after the Fall.

FEATURES

- The reef stonefish is usually brown or gray with patches of yellow, red, or orange. It is extremely well camouflaged, looking like an encrusted rock or lump of coral. This camouflage allows the stonefish to surprise its prey.

FUN FACTS

- The reef stonefish is probably the most venomous fish in the world. It has 13 spines in its dorsal fin that inject venom into its victim. The venom is a neurotoxin.
- This fish sits quietly on reefs and has been known to inject its toxin into the feet of hapless waders through hypodermic-like hollow dorsal spines. These attacks have been fatal at times.
- Its habit of partially burying itself in the sand makes it virtually invisible.

CLASS: Actinopterygii (ray-finned fishes)
ORDER: Scorpaeniformes (scorpion fishes and sculpins)
FAMILY: Synanceiidae (firefishes, goblinfishes, rockfishes, and scorpionfishes)
GENUS/SPECIES: *Synanceia verrucosa*

Size: Up to 14 in (35 cm)
Diet: Fish and crustaceans
Habitat: On the coral reefs and near rocks in the tropical waters of the Indo-Pacific

REMORA

REMORA

CREATED ON DAY 5

DESIGN

The remora does not have a swim bladder. It was created with a sucking disc on the top of its head so that it can "hitch-hike" rides on other animals to get around the ocean. Without this ride providing swift movement of water over its gills, the remora would quickly perish. Clearly this design feature did not evolve over long periods of time.

FEATURES

- The remora is a drab brown or black color.
- It is a short and thick fish with a long, flattened head.
- The body of the remora is smooth, with small, cycloid scales.

FUN FACTS

- The remora attaches itself to fish (including sharks and rays), sea turtles, and aquatic mammals.
- Some remoras eat parasites that are on the animal, thus benefiting both species.
- Some fishermen use the remora to capture larger fish and sea turtles. They attach a line to the remora's tail and then release the remora because the remora will soon attach itself to a host. The fishermen then carefully pull in both the remora and its larger host.

CLASS:	Actinopterygii (ray-finned fishes)
ORDER:	Perciformes (perch-like fishes)
FAMILY:	Echeneididae (remoras and sharksuckers)
GENUS/SPECIES:	*Remora remora*
Size:	1–3 ft (30–90 cm)
Habitat:	Worldwide in tropical and warm waters

SCRAWLED FILEFISH

SCRAWLED FILEFISH

CREATED ON DAY 5

DESIGN

The scrawled filefish can stand its primary dorsal fin erect to lodge itself into a crack or crevice of a reef. This feature now is used partially as a defense mechanism, making it difficult for predators to remove the filefish to eat it.

FEATURES

- This scrawled filefish has a body coloring from an olive-brown to a pale gray. It has blue lines and dots that are irregularly distributed over its body. Juveniles are yellowish.
- It also has a pronounced, tube-like mouth at the end of its snout.

FUN FACTS

- Years ago, fishermen used filefish skin to light matches because the skin is so rough.
- A filefish will sometimes float in a vertical position to blend in to blades of seagrass and coral whips.
- Most species of filefishes are able to change their color to closely match their surroundings and are fairly secretive.
- The scrawled filefish is also known as the scribbled filefish.

CLASS:	Actinopterygii (ray-finned fishes)
ORDER:	Tetraodontiformes (cowfishes, filefishes, leatherjackets, puffers, triggerfishes, and trunkfishes)
FAMILY:	Monacanthidae (filefishes)
GENUS/SPECIES:	*Aluterus scriptus*
Size:	Average 1–2.5 ft (0.3–0.8 m)
Depth:	10-400 ft (4–120 m)
Diet:	Seagrasses, hydrozoans, gorgonians, and tunicates
Habitat:	Coastal waters of Western Atlantic, Eastern Atlantic, Eastern Pacific, and Western Indo-Pacific

SEA DRAGON

SEA DRAGON

CREATED ON DAY 5

DESIGN

The sea dragon has an interesting design. It lacks a caudal fin, and has bony plates covering its body. These characteristics restrict its mobility, but the bony plates provide great protection from possible predators. Because of this protection as well as its great camouflage, the sea dragon does not have many predators.

FEATURES

- The sea dragon has elaborate skin filaments that hang from its head, body, and tail.
- The appendages of the leafy sea dragon are usually a shade of green or yellow, and the appendages of the weedy sea dragon are purple with a black border.

FUN FACTS

- Don't be fooled by the delicate appearance of this creature. It is covered in hard plates and has sharp spines.
- The male sea dragon has a brood patch on his tail on which he incubates fertilized eggs for 4–6 weeks.
- To eat, this creature sucks plankton and tiny crustaceans into its tube-like snout.
- These creatures are rarely seen as most are small and inconspicuous bottom dwellers.

CLASS: Actinopterygii (ray-finned fishes)
ORDER: Syngnathiformes (pipefishes and seahorses)
FAMILY: Syngnathidae (pipefishes and seahorses)
GENUS/SPECIES: *Phycodurus eques* (leafy sea dragon) and *Phyllopteryx taeniolatus* (weedy sea dragon)

Size: Up to 18 in (45 cm)
Depth: Most common in depths of 10 to 165 ft (3–50 m)
Diet: Shrimp, sea lice, and larval fish
Habitat: In temperate waters around Australia among the kelp reefs

SEAHORSE

SEAHORSE

CREATED ON DAY 5

DESIGN

The male of all seahorse species carries the fertilized eggs in a brood pouch until they are ready to hatch. During this time, an amazing change is occurring. When the young are first developing, the placental-like fluid provides the fertilized eggs with nutrition and oxygen. Later in their development, this fluid changes its chemical content, which helps the unborn young become familiar with the seawater. This chemical change was not the result of chance, random processes but was the creative design of almighty God.

FEATURES

- The body of the seahorse is similar to the leafy and weedy sea dragons. It is covered with bony plates and has a tube-like snout.
- The seahorse is well camouflaged in its habitat.

FUN FACTS

- The genus name *Hippocampus* is the Greek's description of a mythical god that was half-horse and half-fish.
- Some seahorse species can change their color and/or pattern to help them blend into their surroundings.
- The seahorse can move its eyes independently of one another.

CLASS:	Actinopterygii (ray-finned fishes)
ORDER:	Syngnathiformes (pipefishes and sea horses)
FAMILY:	Syngnathidae (pipefishes and sea horses)
GENUS:	*Hippocampus*
SPECIES:	About 35 species
Size:	0.4–11.8 in (1–30 cm)
Depth:	0–26 ft (0–8 m); maximum depth of 180 ft (55 m)
Diet:	Zooplankton, small crustaceans, and larval fishes
Habitat:	Shallow temperate and tropical waters worldwide

SMOOTH TRUNKFISH

SMOOTH TRUNKFISH

CREATED ON DAY 5

DESIGN

The smooth trunkfish "blows" jets of water at the seafloor to uncover organisms that are hidden. How did the fish know to do this? The information was given to this creature by its Creator.

FEATURES

- The smooth trunkfish has a box-like shape.
- Its background color is brown with white spots and a hint of yellow in the middle of its sides.

FUN FACTS

- The body of the trunkfish is enclosed by modified scales that are more like bony plates.
- The surface of the plates is often rough.
- The male trunkfish has a harem of females in its large territory.
- It is a slow-moving diurnal predator.

CLASS:	Actinopterygii (ray-finned fishes)
ORDER:	Tetraodontiformes (cowfishes, filefishes, leatherjackets, puffers, triggerfishes, and trunkfishes)
FAMILY:	Ostraciidae (boxfishes, cowfishes, and trunkfishes)
GENUS/SPECIES:	*Lactophrys triqueter*
Size:	6–12 in (15–30.5 cm)
Diet:	Mollusks, crustaceans, worms, and sponges
Habitat:	Common in the waters of the Caribbean Sea and the Gulf of Mexico

SPOTTED GARDEN EEL

SPOTTED GARDEN EEL

CREATED ON DAY 5

DESIGN

Tightening its muscular body to make itself rigid, the spotted garden eel drives its pointy tail deep into the sandy sea floor. The skin in its tail contains a hard substance, so it isn't hurt. Once the eel is deep enough, it wiggles its dorsal fin, pushing sand out of the hole. Slime from the eel's skin cements the walls of its burrow, preventing cave-ins.

FEATURES

- The spotted garden eel resembles a worm with a white body covered in small black spots. There are three prominent black patches located on the body.

FUN FACTS

- When feeding, the spotted garden eel rises out of its burrow, exposing up to two-thirds of its body.
- Each eel lives in a single burrow, which it rarely leaves.
- Several hundred of these creatures may live together in a colony, swaying in the current like blades of seagrass.
- Juveniles are entirely black.
- When disturbed, the spotted garden eel retreats back into its hole.

CLASS:	Actinopterygii (ray-finned fishes)
ORDER:	Aulopiformes (lizardfishes and relatives)
FAMILY:	Congridae (marine eels)
GENUS/SPECIES:	*Heteroconger hassi*
Size:	Up to 16 in (40 cm)
Depth:	23–150 ft (7–45 m)
Diet:	Plankton
Habitat:	Sandy bottoms near coral reefs in Indo-Pacific oceans from the Red Sea to Australasia and in the Pacific from New Caledonia to the Ryukyu Islands

TRUMPETFISH

TRUMPETFISH

CREATED ON DAY 5

DESIGN

The trumpetfish is a sneaky predator. It will sometimes swim slowly and sneak up on its prey, or it may act like a floating stick. This predatory technique likely became part of the trumpetfish's instinct after the Fall when animals began to eat other animals.

FEATURES

- This fish is extremely long and slender.
- It also has a long, tube-like snout into which it sucks its prey.
- The trumpetfish's color varies from dark brown to green.

FUN FACTS

- The trumpetfish can change colors. This ability is used as camouflage and can help it find a mate.
- The male trumpetfish carries the fertilized eggs until they are ready to hatch.
- There are three species of trumpetfishes worldwide.

CLASS:	Actinopterygii (ray-finned fishes)
ORDER:	Syngnathiformes (pipefishes and sea horses)
FAMILY:	Aulostomidae (cornetfishes and trumpetfishes)
GENUS/SPECIES:	*Aulostomus maculatus*
Size:	Less than two ft (0.6 m)
Depth:	10–100 ft (3–30.5 m)
Diet:	Small fish and crustaceans
Habitat:	Coral reefs or lagoons throughout the Indo-Pacific and eastern Pacific

UNICORNFISH

UNICORNFISH

CREATED ON DAY 5

DESIGN

Algae needs an abundance of oxygen and sunlight to thrive, which makes the shallow coral reefs of the tropics a perfect place for algae to multiply. Left undisturbed, algae would soon blanket the coral in a carpet of green and the coral would soon die. To the rescue come algae-eaters like the unicornfish. The mouth of this fish (like other surgeonfishes) is perfectly designed to carefully remove the algae from coral while leaving the coral intact. Its fine row of sharp, small teeth make short work of the algae.

FEATURES

- The unicornfish is easily identified by the bony horn on its forehead, in front of the eyes, though not all species exhibit this horn.
- There are two plates on either side of the tail with razor-sharp spines (scalpels) that are used both offensively and defensively, against one another in struggles for dominance or against predators.
- Unicornfishes come in slender, tubular shapes, as well as the more typical flattened form.

FUN FACTS

- The horn-like appendage between the eyes begins growing when a young fish reaches about 5 in (13 cm) in length, and tends to be a little bigger on males.
- The unicornfish does not use its horn for defense, but rather its sharp tail spines. Biologists are unsure of the purpose of the horn.
- This fish has the amazing ability to change its color almost instantly depending on its environment and its mood.

CLASS:	Actinopterygii (ray-finned fishes)
ORDER:	Perciformes (perch-like fishes)
FAMILY:	Acanthuridae (surgeonfishes and unicornfishes)
GENUS/SPECIES:	*Naso* (19 species)
Size:	Up to 2 ft (61 cm)
Depth:	15–150 ft (5–45 m)
Diet:	Zooplankton and algae
Habitat:	Indo-Pacific; from Hawaii to Indian Ocean, up into the Red Sea

WHITE STURGEON

WHITE STURGEON

CREATED ON DAY 5

DESIGN

By instinct, the white sturgeon spawns in swift-moving water. Evidence shows that spawning under such conditions gives the young the best chance for survival. But how did the white sturgeon know this? This instinct was given to it by its Creator and was not the result of chance, random processes.

FEATURES

- This large fish has a cylindrical body but lacks the small scales of other smaller fishes. Instead it has five rows of scutes along its body.
- The white sturgeon's body is light gray with a white underside, and its scutes are lighter than its body in color.

FUN FACTS

- The white sturgeon has no teeth. It eats by sucking in its food.
- A sturgeon's taste buds are located on the outside of its mouth.
- It is the largest freshwater fish in North America.
- The white sturgeon can live for 100 years or more.
- Other names for this species include Pacific sturgeon, Oregon sturgeon, Columbia sturgeon, and Sacramento sturgeon.

CLASS:	Actinopterygii (ray-finned fishes)
ORDER:	Acipenseriformes (paddlefishes, spoonfishes, and sturgeons)
FAMILY:	Acipenseridae (sturgeons)
GENUS/SPECIES:	*Acipenser transmontanus*

Size:	12.5–20 ft (3.8–6 m)
Weight:	Up to 1,390 lbs (630 kg)
Depth:	1–400 ft (1–122 m)
Diet:	Crustaceans, mollusks, lampreys
Habitat:	Near the shores of the Pacific coast from Alaska to California; migrates inland to spawn

YELLOW PERCH

YELLOW PERCH

CREATED ON DAY 5

DESIGN

Yellow perch are poor swimmers. As a result, these creatures swim in schools of 50–200 fish to protect themselves from predators. Fish very well may have schooled before the Fall of man, but not for defensive reasons. The sheer beauty of a school of fish is reason enough for God to have created this way.

FEATURES

- The adult yellow perch is golden, while the juvenile is whiter.
- This fish has darker bars that run vertically on its body.

FUN FACTS

- Sometimes schools of yellow perch are separated into male and female schools.
- This is a highly prized food fish in North America.
- Yellow perch, as well as many minnows, scatter adhesive eggs over beds of aquatic plants.

CLASS:	Actinopterygii (ray-finned fishes)
ORDER:	Perciformes (perch-like fishes)
FAMILY:	Percidae (perches and true perches)
GENUS/SPECIES:	*Perca flavescens*
Size:	4–10 in (10–25.4 cm)
Diet:	Insects, invertebrates, fish, and fish eggs
Habitat:	Lakes and large rivers of North America, from central Canada to New Brunswick and down to South Carolina and west to Kansas

YELLOW TANG

YELLOW TANG

CREATED ON DAY 5

DESIGN

The yellow tang is designed with sharp spines near its tail to help protect itself against predators and to anchor it to the rocks while sleeping. The mouth is perfectly designed to eat the algae on rocks. These designs were not the results of random, chance processes; they reflect the provision and creativity of its Creator.

FEATURES

- This small, thin fish is bright yellow.
- It has a long snout-like mouth.

FUN FACTS

- The yellow tang is also called the Pacific tang.
- During the night, its color fades. Its bright yellow color returns rapidly when the fish wakes up.
- The yellow tang is a popular aquarium fish and the top marine fish export from Hawaii.
- Group-spawning as well as pair-spawning by territorial males has been observed with this species.

CLASS:	Actinopterygii (ray-finned fishes)
ORDER:	Perciformes (perch-like fishes)
FAMILY:	Acanthuridae (surgeonfishes and tangs)
GENUS/SPECIES:	*Zebrasoma flavescens*
Size:	3–5 in (7.6–13 cm)
Depth:	7–150 ft (2.1–45 m)
Diet:	Browses on filamentous algae
Habitat:	In the reefs in the Pacific and Indian Oceans, west of Hawaii to East Africa

ZEBRAFISH

ZEBRAFISH

CREATED ON DAY 5

DESIGN

The Creator gave the zebrafish the ability to regenerate its skin, fins, heart, and even its brain in larval stages. Zebrafish also seem to have the ability to regenerate photoreceptors and retinal neurons following injury.

FEATURES

- The zebrafish is named for its five uniform, horizontal blue stripes on the side of its body, all of which extend from the gill cover back to the tail.
- The male is torpedo shaped and has gold stripes between its blue stripes; the female has a larger, whitish belly and has silver stripes instead of gold.

FUN FACTS

- The embryonic development of the zebrafish is very rapid. In the first 24 hours after fertilization, all major organs form and within three days the fish hatches and starts looking for food.
- The zebrafish is one of the few animals that have been flown into space.
- The family to which the zebrafish belongs (minnows and carps) is the largest of all fish families, with over 2,000 species.

CLASS: Actinopterygii (ray-finned fishes)
ORDER: Cypriniformes (carps)
FAMILY: Cyprinidae (minnows and carps)
GENUS/SPECIES: *Danio rerio*

Size: Up to 1.5 in (4 cm)
Diet: Worms, small crustaceans, insect larvae
Habitat: Streams, canals, ponds, and rice fields in India, Pakistan, Bangladesh, Nepal, and Myanmar

BLACKTIP REEF SHARK

BLACKTIP REEF SHARK

CREATED ON DAY 5

DESIGN

The blacktip reef shark is one of the only sharks that can jump fully out of the water. Scientists are still studying the purpose of this behavior, but they think it could be to give the shark a look at its surroundings, to show dominance over another, to court a mate, or to remove parasites from its skin. No matter what the reason, how did the shark know to do this? The information for such behavior was given to this creature by its Creator.

FEATURES

- The blacktip reef shark has black tips on its fins, a white band on the dorsal fin, and a light streak on each side.
- This shark is a sleek, active swimmer.

FUN FACTS

- The young of this shark are called "pups," and two to four are born per litter.
- The Australian Aborigines eat this shark, and other people use this shark's liver oil for various purposes.
- The blacktip reef shark is normally very shy and easily frightened.
- On rare occasions it has been known to bite waders, but these are probably cases of mistaken identity.

CLASS:	Chondrichthyes (cartilaginous fish—sharks, skates, and rays)
ORDER:	Carcharhiniformes (ground sharks)
FAMILY:	Carcharhinidae (requiem sharks)
GENUS/SPECIES:	*Carcharhinus melanopterus*
Size:	Up to 6 ft (1.8 m)
Weight:	31 lbs (14 kg)
Depth:	Commonly up to 250 ft (75 m)
Diet:	Reef fish, squid, octopuses, shrimp, sea snakes
Habitat:	Shallow, tropical waters of the Indo-Pacific region

BLUE SHARK

BLUE SHARK

CREATED ON DAY 5

DESIGN

The blue shark's sleek, tapered body makes it a graceful swimmer. Its elongated tail provides swimming power as it moves side-to-side. This shark is among the fastest swimming of the sharks and probably among the fastest swimming of all fish. Estimates of its speed vary, but some say that it can swim at about 60 miles per hour (97 km/h).

FEATURES

- This shark is deep blue on its dorsal side, lighter blue on its sides, and white on its belly. This type of coloration is called "counter-shading."
- The blue shark has a relatively long snout and extremely long pectoral fins.
- It also has very large circular eyes.

FUN FACTS

- The blue shark has large litters of 25 to over 100 young.
- It is the world's most wide-ranging shark, being found in all temperate and tropical seas, from 50° N to 40° S latitude.
- This species is an open ocean (pelagic) shark.

CLASS:	Chondrichthyes (cartilaginous fish—sharks, skates, and rays)
ORDER:	Carcharhiniformes (ground sharks)
FAMILY:	Carcharhinidae (requiem sharks)
GENUS/SPECIES:	*Prionace glauca*
Size:	Average 6–8 ft (1.8–2.4 m)
Weight:	150–175 lbs (59–79 kg)
Depth:	Down to 1,150 ft (350 m)
Diet:	Fish, squid, cuttlefishes, octopuses
Habitat:	Worldwide in tropical and temperate waters

BONNETHEAD SHARK

BONNETHEAD SHARK

CREATED ON DAY 5

DESIGN

An unusual feature of this shark is its ability to produce a special fluid called "cerebrospinal fluid." It is thought that the shark uses this fluid to communicate with other sharks in its area. This special ability shows the creativity and ability of its Creator.

FEATURES

- This shark is a grayish-brown color on its dorsal side with a lighter underside.
- It has small teeth in the front of its mouth and broad teeth in the back.

FUN FACTS

- The bonnethead shark is also called the shovelhead shark.
- This is the smallest shark in its family.
- It inhabits waters that are usually warmer than 70°F (21°C).
- During the summer, the bonnethead shark is common in the waters of the Carolinas and Georgia.

CLASS:	Chondrichthyes (cartilaginous fish—sharks, skates, and rays)
ORDER:	Carcharhiniformes (ground sharks)
FAMILY:	Sphyrnidae (bonnethead sharks, hammerhead sharks, and scoophead sharks)
GENUS/SPECIES:	*Sphyrna tiburo*
Size:	Up to 5 ft (1.6 m)
Depth:	Commonly found 33–82 ft (10–25 m)
Diet:	Crustaceans, mollusks, small fish
Habitat:	Waters of the Western Atlantic, from Rhode Island and North Carolina to the Caribbean Sea and southern Brazil; waters of the Eastern Pacific, from Southern California to Ecuador

GREAT HAMMERHEAD SHARK

GREAT HAMMERHEAD SHARK

CREATED ON DAY 5

DESIGN

The most striking design feature is the shape of the great hammerhead shark's head. It was designed by the Creator, but its purpose is not fully understood. Some scientists speculate it maximizes the area of sensory organs that are used to detect thermal, chemical, and physical changes, as well as electrical fields of prey.

FEATURES

- The most distinguishing feature of the great hammerhead shark is the shape of its almost rectangular head. The anterior margin is nearly straight.
- Its eyes are located at each end of its hammer-like head.
- The hammerhead shark varies in color from a dark olive to a brownish-gray on the upper half. The underside is white.

FUN FACTS

- A newborn great hammerhead shark's head is a round shape, but it will change to the unique "hammer" shape as it becomes an adult.
- The great hammerhead shark is the largest of the nine hammerhead species.
- The nutrition of the embryos is by a placental-like arrangement, including an umbilical cord.
- The number of young varies from 12 to 40.

CLASS:	Chondrichthyes (cartilaginous fish—sharks, skates, and rays)
ORDER:	Carcharhiniformes (ground sharks)
FAMILY:	Sphyrnidae (bonnethead sharks, hammerhead sharks, and scoophead sharks)
GENUS/SPECIES:	*Sphyrna mokarran*
Size:	13–20 ft (4–6 m)
Weight:	Average 945 lbs (430 kg)
Diet:	Fish, squid, octopuses, crustaceans
Habitat:	Open and shallow tropical waters worldwide

LEOPARD SHARK

LEOPARD SHARK

CREATED ON DAY 5

DESIGN

Research indicates that the red blood cells of the leopard shark are smaller and more numerous than the red blood cells of other sharks. This may provide the leopard shark the ability to more easily absorb oxygen from the water. It also has electroreceptors in its snout to help it locate buried prey, such as worms.

FEATURES

- The leopard shark is most distinguished by the dark barbs on its dorsal fins.
- A young leopard has dark patches across its back and spots on its sides. As it ages it will usually lose these dark markings.
- Its body is long and slender and the adult has broad triangular pectoral fins.

FUN FACTS

- The leopard shark is also called a cat shark.
- This shark is generally considered to be non-threatening to humans, and is most commonly found in muddy bays, including estuaries and lagoons.
- This shark is used for human consumption.
- The leopard shark is ovoviviparous and has four to 29 pups per litter.

CLASS:	Chondrichthyes (cartilaginous fish—sharks, skates, and rays)
ORDER:	Carcharhiniformes (ground sharks)
FAMILY:	Triakidae (houndsharks, smooth-hounds, topes, and whiskery sharks)
GENUS/SPECIES:	*Triakis semifasciata*
Size:	Up to 7 ft (2.1 m)
Weight:	42 lbs (19 kg)
Diet:	Crustaceans, fish, worms, clams, octopuses
Habitat:	Shallow waters of the Pacific Ocean from Oregon to Baja, California

MANTA RAY

MANTA RAY

CREATED ON DAY 5

DESIGN

During embryonic development, part of the tissue that becomes the pectoral fins of the manta ray breaks away and moves forward, surrounding the mouth. This structure develops into horns. These flexible horns are used to direct plankton and water into the manta's very broad and wide mouth. To make it more streamlined when swimming, it is able to curl its horns up.

FEATURES

- The manta ray is most easily recognized by its large pectoral "wings."
- It also has "horns" that protrude from either side of its head.
- The manta ray is usually black above and white below, but can be blue on its back.

FUN FACTS

- This ray has a number of other names, including Atlantic manta, devil ray, devilfish, and giant manta.
- The manta ray is the largest of the rays.
- This species is completely harmless, though its extremely large size can be very intimidating.

CLASS:	Chondrichthyes (cartilaginous fish—sharks, skates, and rays)
ORDER:	Rajiformes (rays, sawfishes, and skates)
FAMILY:	Mobulidae (devil rays and manta rays)
GENUS/SPECIES:	*Manta birostris*
Size:	Wingspan 17–22 ft (5.2–6.7 m)
Weight:	2,640–3,080 lbs (1,200–1,400 kg)
Depth:	Near the surface, down to 395 ft (120 m)
Diet:	Shrimp, plankton, small fish
Habitat:	Tropical and temperate waters near the coasts of the oceans

NURSE SHARK

NURSE SHARK

CREATED ON DAY 5

DESIGN

Unlike most sharks, the nurse shark does not have to constantly move water across its gills to breathe. The nurse shark can remain motionless on the seafloor because of its ability to pump water across its gills. It does this by opening and closing its mouth. This design was given to the nurse shark by its Creator.

FEATURES

- This sluggish shark has a yellowish-brown to dark brown body that is relatively flat.
- Some have small dark spots or patches on their bodies.
- The most distinguishing feature of the nurse shark is the barbels that hang down from the shark's jaw. Barbels are fleshy appendages that house the taste buds. They are used to search for food in murky water.

FUN FACTS

- Its teeth are fan-shaped, which helps it crush crustaceans, which it eats.
- Nurse sharks will pile on top of one another on the seafloor when they are resting.
- The nurse shark does not migrate; it simply adapts by limiting its activity.
- Most sharks and rays have a unique ability to regulate incoming light levels. The constricted, light-adapted pupil takes the shape of an oblique slit in this species.

CLASS:	Chondrichthyes (cartilaginous fish—sharks, skates, and rays)
ORDER:	Orectolobiformes (carpet sharks)
FAMILY:	Ginglymostomatidae (nurse sharks)
GENUS/SPECIES:	*Ginglymostoma cirratum*
Size:	Average 10 ft (3 m)
Diet:	Shrimp, squid, fish, octopus, crabs, sea urchins, corals
Habitat:	Shallow tropical and subtropical waters of the Western Atlantic, Eastern Atlantic, and Eastern Pacific Oceans

STINGRAY

STINGRAY

CREATED ON DAY 5

DESIGN

The eyes of the stingray are on the top of its body, while its mouth is on the underside of its body. This makes it impossible for a stingray to see what it is eating. Therefore, the stingray relies on its keen sense of smell and the electroreceptors that help it identify its food.

FEATURES

- The stingray is most recognized for its large, wing-like pectoral fins that make this creature look like it is flying through the water.
- A stingray's coloring often reflects the shading of the seafloor. Some species are spotted or shaded.
- The stinger of the stingray is actually an extension of its spine. The entire spine is covered with a layer of skin where venom is concentrated.
- The stingray has a greatly depressed disc (roundish, flat body).

FUN FACTS

- Ancient Greek dentists used the venom in the stingray's spine as an anesthetic.
- If the stingray loses its stinger, it can grow another one in its place.
- This species lacks dorsal fins.
- The stingray respires ("breathes") by drawing water through a small hole, or spiracle, behind each eye and expelling it through gill slits located under the disc.

CLASS:	Chondrichthyes (cartilaginous fish—sharks, skates, and rays)
ORDER:	Myliobatidiformes (rays)
FAMILY:	Dasyatididae (stingrays and whiprays)
GENUS/SPECIES:	70 species in 6 genera
Size:	Up to 6.5 ft (2 m), without the tail
Weight:	Up to 790 lbs (350 kg)
Diet:	Worms, carrion, squid, crustaceans
Habitat:	Common in tropical coastal waters worldwide; freshwater species in Asia, Africa, and North America

TIGER SHARK

TIGER SHARK

CREATED ON DAY 5

DESIGN

Like most sharks, the tiger shark has an incredible sense of smell. This feature allows the tiger shark to smell small traces of blood, and its electroreceptors allow the shark to locate and track prey, even in the dark. These features were not used in hunting in the original created kind, since all creatures were created to eat only plants.

FEATURES

- The tiger shark's coloring varies from bluish or greenish gray to black on its back and from light gray to dingy yellow on its belly.
- The tiger shark's tail has a large upper lobe, which delivers the power it needs for slow cruising or sudden bursts of speed.
- A young pup has spotted markings across its back that fades as it ages.

FUN FACTS

- These sharks eat almost anything. Things found in their stomachs have included coal, dogs, overcoats, a drum, a chicken coop, and bottles. If they become too full with items that they cannot digest, they will throw up everything to make room for more. They can eat toxic fish such as trunkfishes and porcupinefishes with no ill effects.
- The tiger shark has a special gill slit (a spiracle) behind its eyes that provides oxygen flow directly to the eyes and brain.
- There is little doubt that the tiger shark is the most dangerous animal inhabiting coral reefs.
- This shark is ovoviviparous and may have up to 80 or more pups per litter.

CLASS:	Chondrichthyes (cartilaginous fish—sharks, skates, and rays)
ORDER:	Carcharhiniformes (ground sharks)
FAMILY:	Carcharhinidae (requiem sharks)
GENUS/SPECIES:	*Galeocerdo cuvier*
Size:	10–18 ft (3–5.5 m)
Weight:	900–1,500 lbs (408–680 kg)
Diet:	Crabs, lobsters, squid, fish, porpoises, turtles, marine birds and mammals
Habitat:	Worldwide in tropical and sub-tropical waters

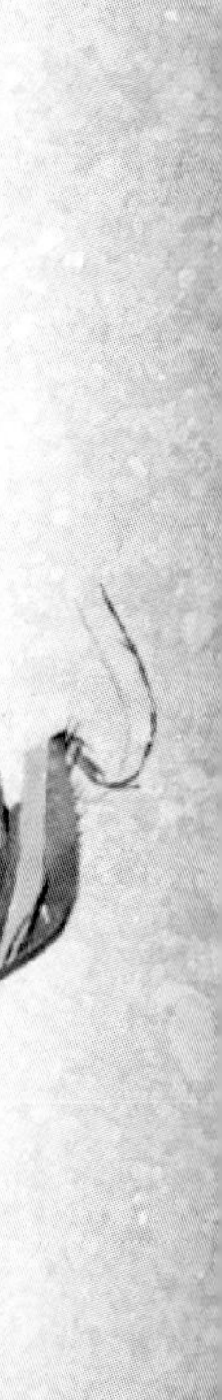

WHALE SHARK

WHALE SHARK

CREATED ON DAY 5

DESIGN

Despite the immense size of this creature, it does not need to be feared by man; it feeds mostly on zooplankton and small fish. It has gill rakers in its mouth that filter the food from the water it has taken in. The water then passes through the gill slits, and the food is swallowed. It is said that the whale shark can filter as much as 1,500 gallons (6,000 ℓ) of water every hour when feeding.

FEATURES

- The whale shark is dark gray or greenish gray from its back to the middle of its sides. Its belly is off-white.
- White or light yellow spots and lines are also distinguishing features of the whale shark.
- Whale sharks can grow to a length of 60 ft (18 m).

FUN FACTS

- The whale shark is the largest fish in the world.
- It can reach up to 150 years of age.
- The whale shark's mouth can open up to 5 ft (1.5 m) wide and can contain up to 300 rows of tiny teeth.

CLASS:	Chondrichthyes (cartilaginous fish—sharks, skates, and rays)
ORDER:	Orectolobiformes (carpet sharks)
FAMILY:	Rhincodontidae
GENUS/SPECIES:	*Rhincodon typus*
Size:	30–46 ft (12–20 m); females are larger than males.
Weight:	Up to 20 tons
Diet:	Plankton, small fish
Habitat:	In the warm waters around the equator worldwide, except for the Mediterranean Sea

WHITETIP REEF SHARK

WHITETIP REEF SHARK

CREATED ON DAY 5

DESIGN

The whitetip reef shark is a nocturnal creature. Because of this feature, this shark relies heavily on its keen eyesight. Its eyes are large and oval, which help the shark see well in dim light. It also uses its strong chemosensory and electroreceptor systems to help it locate prey in the dark. These features were not used by the original created kind to hunt prey, but became useful hunting tools once animals began to hunt other animals after the Fall of man.

FEATURES

- The distinguishing feature of this shark is the white coloring on the tip of its fins.
- Its belly is white and the rest of its body is gray-brown.
- It has a blunt snout

FUN FACTS

- The tough skin of the whitetip reef shark is perfect for its coral habitat.
- This shark can remain motionless on the seafloor because it has the ability to pump water over its gills without moving.
- This shark has been observed at a depth of 400 ft (122 m) from a submersible.
- A whitetip reef shark often returns to its favorite resting site at the same time each day, often for several years.

CLASS:	Chondrichthyes (cartilaginous fish—sharks, skates, and rays)
ORDER:	Carcharhiniformes (ground sharks)
FAMILY:	Carcharhinidae (requiem sharks)
GENUS/SPECIES:	*Triaenodon obesus*
Size:	Average 5.5 ft (1.7 m)
Weight:	Average 44 lbs (20 kg)
Depth:	Most common between 26–130 ft (8–40 m)
Diet:	Fish, crustaceans, octopuses
Habitat:	Shallow, tropical waters around the coral reefs in the Indian and Pacific Oceans

ZEBRA SHARK

ZEBRA SHARK

CREATED ON DAY 5

DESIGN

Like other bottom-dwelling sharks, the zebra shark can pump water over its gills. This ability was a provision within this creature's original created kind.

FEATURES

- This shark is cylindrical with a long tail and broad head.
- Its gray body is covered with dark brown spots.
- The young zebra shark has stripes and a darker body. As it grows, the zebra shark loses its stripes and develops spots.

FUN FACTS

- The zebra shark is oviparous. The pups hatch from eggs that are left on rocks at the bottom of reefs.
- This shark's tail is sometimes as long as, if not longer than, its body, and it lacks a distinct lower lobe.
- This shark is commonly, and incorrectly, referred to as a leopard shark because of the pattern of leopard-like spots that develop with maturity.

CLASS:	Chondrichthyes (cartilaginous fish—sharks, skates, and rays)
ORDER:	Orecctolobiformes (carpet sharks)
FAMILY:	Stegastomatidae (zebra sharks)
GENUS/SPECIES:	*Stegastoma fasciatum* (or *Stegostoma varium*)
Size:	8–10 ft (2.4–3 m)
Depth:	Up to 203 ft (62 m)
Diet:	Mollusks and crustaceans
Habitat:	Indian Ocean, west Pacific Ocean; abundant in Australian coastal waters

AMERICAN LOBSTER

AMERICAN LOBSTER

CREATED ON DAY 5

DESIGN

The lobster has a unique design. Its mouth is used for much more than just eating. If a lobster loses its claws and legs, it will use its mouth to pull itself around. The lobster does not chew its food; instead it has three grinders in its stomach that process the food. It uses its long antennae to feel the surrounding area, and its short antennules provide its sense of smell, which helps the lobster locate prey, predators, mates, and opponents. These designs all help the lobster survive.

FEATURES

- The American lobster is normally a shade of reddish-brown.
- Most people recognize the lobster by its two large front claws. These are two of their ten legs, but they are not used for walking. One claw is used to grasp something for a long time, and the other one is the pincher that is used to grab something quickly.

FUN FACTS

- The largest American lobster weighed 44 lbs (20 kg).
- It is also known as the northern lobster or the Maine lobster.
- Some genetic defects have resulted in blue, yellow, split-color, and albino lobsters.
- The American lobster is aggressive and will fight for the possession of rocky cave shelters.

CLASS:	Malacostraca (crabs, krill, pill bugs, shrimp, and relatives)
ORDER:	Decapoda (crabs, shrimp, and relatives)
FAMILY:	Nephropidae (clawed lobsters)
GENUS/SPECIES:	*Homarus americanus*
Size:	8–24 in (20–60 cm)
Weight:	1–9 lbs (0.5–4 kg)
Diet:	Fish, crab, mussels, clams, starfish, sea urchins
Habitat:	Shallow waters of the North American coasts

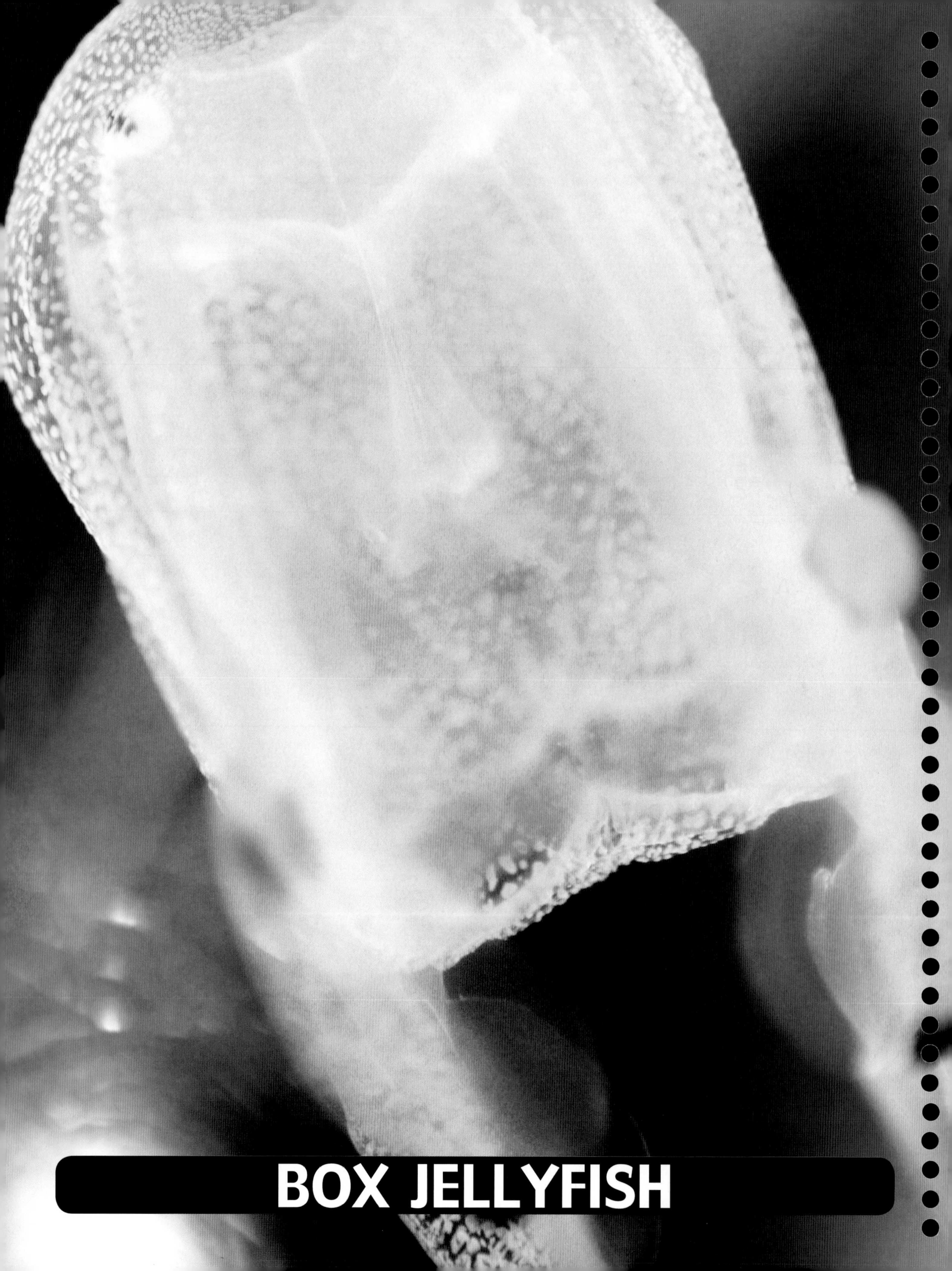

BOX JELLYFISH

BOX JELLYFISH

CREATED ON DAY 5

DESIGN

The box jellyfish is able to see through four sets of eyes, one at the center of each side of the bell, each set clustered in a club-shaped structure called the rhopalium. Each set actually consists of six eyes: four simple pigmented pits with photoreceptors and two complex camera eyes, one pointing up and one pointing down, each with a cornea, lens, and retina. Scientists are not sure how the animal processes the visual information since it has no brain. Certainly, God designed this "primitive" animal with amazing capabilities that defy any evolutionary explanation.

FEATURES

- Box jellyfish are pale blue, transparent, and bell or cube shaped with four distinct sides.
- The box jellyfish has a group of 15 tentacles at each corner of its body, with up to 5,000 stinging cells each.

FUN FACTS

- Box jellies are also called sea wasps and marine stingers.
- The box jellyfish is not a true jellyfish
- The box jellyfish is one of the most venomous creatures in the ocean. Its sting can kill a human in just a few minutes, its venom attacking the nervous system.
- Some sea turtles can eat the box jellyfish without being affected by its sting.

CLASS:	Cubozoa (sea wasps or box jellyfish)
ORDER:	Cubomedusae
FAMILY:	Chirodropidae
GENUS/SPECIES:	*Chironex fleckeri*
Size:	Up to 10 in (25 cm); tentacles up to 10 ft (3 m)
Depth:	Near the surface
Diet:	Shrimp and small fish
Habitat:	Open tropical waters of southwest Pacific and eastern Indian Oceans

CHAMBERED NAUTILUS

CHAMBERED NAUTILUS

CREATED ON DAY 5

DESIGN

To keep itself afloat and upright, the chambered nautilus has a tube called a siphuncle that runs down the center of each chamber and releases a gas, maintaining a density close to that of sea water. This allows the chambered nautilus to swim about with a minimum of effort. The information for this design was part of God's provision for this creature at its creation; this feature did not evolve.

FEATURES

- The spiral-shaped shell of the nautilus has a pattern of brown and white.
- The creature creates up to 30 different chambers within its shell that it will occupy as it grows. A tough hood protects the nautilus where its body connects to its shell.

FUN FACTS

- This species is probably the most common nautilus.
- The chambered nautilus also has small tentacles that it uses to swim or pull itself along rocks.
- In the daytime it descends about 2,000 ft (610 m) into the deep and at night it rises to a depth of 300–500 ft (90–150 m) to feed.
- The nautilus has an unusually long life span for a cephalopod; it may live for more than 15 years.

CLASS:	Cephalopoda (octopuses and squids)
ORDER:	Nautilida (nautilus)
FAMILY:	Nautilidae (chambered nautilus)
GENUS/SPECIES:	*Nautilus pompilius*
Size:	Up to 8 in (20 cm) long
Depth:	Up to 1,640 ft (500 m)
Diet:	Crabs and shrimp
Habitat:	In the water column where the slopes of coral reefs descend into deep waters

CHITON

CHITON

CREATED ON DAY 5

DESIGN

The chiton is well-designed for its habitat and diet. The low, curved shape of the chiton and its strong foot help it stay attached to rocks even in the heaviest of seas. The chiton's mouth has a tongue-like structure called a radula, which has numerous rows of about 17 teeth each. The teeth are coated with magnetite, a mineral that hardens the teeth. The radula is used to scrape microscopic algae off the substratum.

FEATURES

- The body of a chiton is low and oval. It is covered by a shell consisting of eight arching and overlapping plates.
- The chiton has a muscular foot that clings to rocks and allows it to creep slowly.

FUN FACTS

- Chitons are also called sea cradles and loricates.
- A chiton has only one foot.
- The chiton has no eyes, but it does have light-sensitive organs in its shell.
- When dislodged, a chiton rolls itself into a ball.
- The chiton's radula is sharper than your average kitchen knife.

CLASS:	Mollusca (mollusks)
CLASS:	Polyplacophora (chitons)
ORDER:	Neoloricata (chitons)
FAMILY:	Almost 1000 species in seven families
Size:	2–13 in (5–33 cm)
Diet:	Algae, diatoms, bacteria
Habitat:	Along seashores worldwide; most common in cooler waters

CLEANER SHRIMP

CLEANER SHRIMP

CREATED ON DAY 5

DESIGN

The role of the cleaner shrimp is truly unique. Many species of fish, including some species of eels, allow the cleaner shrimp to clean parasites from inside their mouths. The cleaner shrimp is in no danger of being eaten when it enters the fishes' mouths to clean. This symbiotic relationship is part of God's provision for His sea-dwelling creatures.

FEATURES

- This shrimp is known for the orange coloring along its sides and the long red stripe on its dorsal side that is bisected by a narrow, white band. It also has white spots on its tail and three pairs of white antennae.

FUN FACTS

- This shrimp may also be called the Pacific cleaner shrimp, the white-banded cleaner shrimp, and the skunk cleaner shrimp.
- In many coral reefs, cleaner shrimp congregate at cleaning stations where fish come to be cleaned of bacteria and dead skin.
- This is a popular member of home aquariums where it is easy to keep.

CLASS:	Malacostraca (crabs, krill, pill bugs, shrimp, and relatives)
ORDER:	Decapoda
FAMILY:	Hippolytidae
GENUS/SPECIES:	*Lysmata amboinensis*
Size:	About 2.4 in (6 cm)
Diet:	Dead and diseased skin, bacteria, and parasites from their "customers"
Habitat:	Red Sea and tropical waters of the Indo-Pacific region

COMMON LIMPET

COMMON LIMPET

CREATED ON DAY 5

DESIGN

The shape of the limpet varies. The closer the limpet is to the water, the flatter and smaller its shell. The farther the limpet is from the water, the wider and taller its shell. This design is an adaptation that God programmed into the species' DNA for survival. Without this adaptation, the waves would beat against and be more likely to pull away a tall, wide limpet close to the water. This is an example of adaptation, not evolution.

FEATURES

- The common limpet has a cone-like shell that protects it from predators and from the environment.
- The limpet travels across the rocks by contracting its single foot.
- Its shell is gray to dirty white, often with yellow to red markings. The interior of the shell is gray-green.

FUN FACTS

- The limpet travels across the rocks to find food, but it has a certain spot that it has ground into the rock as its anchor spot. When the limpet moves from this spot, it leaves a trail of mucus to follow back to its anchor spot.
- It is found on exposed coastlines as well as quiet bays.
- This species is moderately territorial, showing some aggression toward other individuals of the same species.

CLASS:	Gastropoda (gastropods, slugs, and snails)
ORDER:	Patellogastropoda (limpets)
FAMILY:	Patellidae (marine limpets)
GENUS/SPECIES:	*Patella vulgata*
Size:	Up to 2.4 in (6 cm) in diameter
Diet:	Algae, diatoms, and blue-green algae
Habitat:	Rocks on shores of Northeastern Atlantic coast, from the Arctic Circle to Portugal

COMMON MUSSEL

COMMON MUSSEL

CREATED ON DAY 5

DESIGN

Common mussels live in large colonies and release their gametes (eggs and sperm) synchronously (at the same time) in the water column for maximum fertilization. The mussel was also created with the ability to make extremely tough fibers, called byssus threads, that it uses to attach itself to other things. These threads resemble soft rubber at one end and rigid nylon at the other and are 5 times tougher than a human tendon.

FEATURES

- The shell of the common mussel has two halves (hence its name "bivalve"), both similar in shape. After the shell has been opened, a large closing muscle and four pairs of gills become visible.
- It is a filter feeder and uses its cilia to funnel sea water into its mouth opening, where it filters minute food particles for digestion.

FUN FACTS

- This creature is also called the blue mussel.
- The common mussel can process 10–18 gallons (45–70 ℓ) of water a day; it absorbs oxygen from the water that passes over its gills.
- The common mussel can defend itself from predator snails by tying them down with its byssus threads.
- This species is commonly farmed and harvested for food throughout the world.

CLASS:	Bivalvia (bivalves and clams)
ORDER:	Mytiloida (mussels)
FAMILY:	Mytilidae (mussels)
GENUS/SPECIES:	*Mytilus edulis*
Size:	2–5 in (5–13 cm)
Diet:	Organic matter and phytoplankton
Habitat:	Coasts and estuaries of north and southeastern Atlantic Ocean, and the northeastern and southwestern Pacific Ocean

COMMON SAND DOLLAR

COMMON SAND DOLLAR

CREATED ON DAY 5

DESIGN

Small but numerous spines of the common sand dollar are its primary tool for burrowing within the upper few centimeters of sandy ocean bottoms. Other specialized spines hold sand and debris aloft while food particles are ingested.

FEATURES

- The sand dollar's test, or skeleton, is round and disc-like, and is covered with deep reddish-purple spines. The sand dollar loses its purple color when it is washed ashore.
- As with other sand dollars, the common sand dollar has five petal-like furrows or pores on its test. These are used to move sea water into its internal water-vascular system, which allows for movement.

FUN FACTS

- Its shell is actually called a "test" since it is not a true shell.
- The common sand dollar buries itself in the sand for food and protection.
- The best time to collect sand dollars on the beach is after a heavy storm.

CLASS:	Echinoidea (heart urchins, sand dollars, and sea urchins)
ORDER:	Clypeasteroida (sand dollars)
FAMILY:	Echinarachniidae
GENUS/SPECIES:	*Echinarachnius parma*
Size:	Average 3 in (7.6 cm) in diameter
Diet:	Crustacean larvae, organic matter, diatoms, algae
Habitat:	Native to the Northern Hemisphere in the sandy bottoms of the coasts

CORAL

CREATED ON DAY 5

DESIGN

Scientists have discovered that coral has layers, and some scientists have measured these layers claiming that they show slow growth over long periods of time. However, it has been shown that coral can grow quickly. With this knowledge, even the "oldest" reefs would only be a few thousand years old. This is consistent with a young earth, created only about 6,000 years ago.

FEATURES

- Coral colonies grow in many shapes and come in many colors; there are three kinds of coral reefs: simple fringing reefs, barrier reefs, and atolls.
- A coral polyp is actually a small, marine invertebrate that lives in a large colony. A polyp looks like a tiny, upside down jellyfish. Some corals have eight tentacles, while others have them in multiples of six.

FUN FACTS

- Coral polyps are connected to one another in large colonies, sharing nutrients and even other organisms in a mutualistic relationship. These large colonies are called reefs.
- Most corals have a beneficial relationship with zooxanthellae (photosynthetic, one-celled algae). The oxygen and sugar produced by the algae within the coral polyp stimulates it to produce calcium carbonate (reef material). The coral produces carbon dioxide and waste products (nutrient-rich fertilizer) that the zooxanthellae use.
- Corals uses their tentacles to trap prey by stinging their prey with cells called nematocysts.

CLASS:	Anthozoa (corals and sea anemones)
SUBCLASS:	Alcyonaria (soft) and Zoantharia (stony)
ORDER:	Nine orders within the two subclasses
GENUS/SPECIES:	Over 5,000 different species
Size:	A few millimeters
Depth:	Up to 200 ft (60 m); one rare species found as deep as 9,800 ft (3,000 m)
Diet:	Zooplankton, small fishes, organic debris
Habitat:	In shallow, warm waters worldwide

CRAYFISH

CRAYFISH

CREATED ON DAY 5

DESIGN

The crayfish must shed its hard exoskeleton in order for its soft body to grow and mature. Baby crayfish molt daily, a pattern that slows down as the crayfish ages. To produce a new exoskeleton, the crayfish ingests calcium, and when the time comes, finds a safe place where it can shed its old shell. The crayfish is then vulnerable to predators until its shell hardens. It will eat its old shell to get the calcium it needs to harden its new exoskeleton. The information programmed in the crayfish's DNA was placed within the original created kind by its Creator.

FEATURES

- The segmented body of the crayfish is usually yellow, green, or dark brown.
- The crayfish has eight jointed walking legs, two pairs of sensory antennae, and two large pincers or claws. It also has several pairs of specialized food-handling "legs," bailers to cycle water over the gills, and five pairs of swimmerets, which are under the abdomen.

FUN FACTS

- The crayfish is commonly referred to as the crawfish, the crawdad, and the mudbug.
- The world's largest species of crayfish can weigh over 8 lbs (3.6 kg).
- All of the "legs" of the crayfish can grow back if they are broken off.
- The walking legs of the crayfish are attached to its gills. When the crayfish walks, its gills move also, helping them absorb more oxygen and eliminate carbon dioxide.

CLASS:	Malacostraca (crabs, krill, pill bugs, shrimp, and relatives)
ORDER:	Decapoda (crabs, shrimp, and relatives)
FAMILY:	Three different families—Astacidae, Cambaridae, and Parastacida
GENUS/SPECIES:	Over 500 species
Size:	Average 3 in (7.5 cm)
Diet:	Snails, algae, insect larvae, worms, and plants
Habitat:	Found mostly in freshwater worldwide; a few live in saltwater

CUTTLEFISH

CUTTLEFISH

CREATED ON DAY 5

DESIGN

The eyes of the cuttlefish are extremely well designed. Its pupils are "w" shaped, and they can focus both forward and backward, giving the cuttlefish all around protection. When frightened or attacked, the cuttlefish releases ink that forms a dense cloud in the water column, allowing it time to escape.

FEATURES

- The thick internal shell of a cuttlefish is called a cuttlebone. It is made of calcium carbonate and contains numerous gas- and/or water-filled chambers.
- The cuttlebone enables the cuttlefish to control its bouyance in the water column.

FUN FACTS

- The cuttlefish is not a fish; it is a mollusk.
- The cuttlefish can rapidly change its skin color to either hide from predators or communicate with other cuttlefish by means of special cells called chromatophores.
- The cuttlefish has three hearts to pump its greenish-blue blood to its gills and body.
- The eggs of the cuttlefish are laid in clumps and are often coated in ink by the mother, camouflaging them.

CLASS:	Cephalopoda (octopuses and squids)
ORDER:	Sepiida (true cuttlefishes)
FAMILY:	Sepiidae (true cuttlefishes)
GENUS/SPECIES:	Over 100 different species in three genera
Size:	Varies depending on species
Diet:	Small fish, crustaceans, and mollusks
Habitat:	Shallow temperate and tropical waters near the shores

FEATHER DUSTER

FEATHER DUSTER

CREATED ON DAY 5

DESIGN

The feather duster hides its body in a tube that it builds between rocks or in crevices on coral or in the sand of the seafloor. When it feels threatened, it will pull its tentacles into the tube in a split second. Its tentacles are used to capture plankton from the currents and for getting oxygen.

FEATURES

- This creature is a segmented sea worm.
- The feather duster has a series of feathery tentacles on its head that it uses to filter nutrients from the water and take in oxygen. These tentacles are called radioles.
- The feather duster lives in a long tube constructed of mud or sand, cemented by a mucus of protein. The mucus also minimizes sand irritation on the animal's body.

FUN FACTS

- This creature is also called a fan worm.
- While most feather dusters are about the size of a pencil lead, some feather duster worms in excess of two feet long with a dense tentacle crown four or more inches across are known in some temperate regions.

CLASS:	Polychaeta (paddle-footed annelids and polychaetes)
ORDER:	Canalipalpata
FAMILY:	Sabellidae
GENUS/SPECIES:	About 130 species in 29 genera
Size:	Average 4 in (10 cm)
Depth:	From 3–65 ft (1–20 m)
Diet:	Plankton and tiny organic particles
Habitat:	Coral reefs of tropical and temperate oceans worldwide

GHOST CRAB

GHOST CRAB

CREATED ON DAY 5

DESIGN

The Creator has given this crab an exceptional ability that helps it survive during the winter. The ghost crab stores oxygen in air sacs near its gills. During its winter hibernation, it uses this stored oxygen while it remains buried in the sand.

FEATURES

- The ghost crab is aptly named. It is a pale, sandy color, making it almost invisible on the sand.
- Its black eyes are held aloft on stalks.
- Like all true crabs, the ghost crab has five pairs of legs, the first of which is a pair of claws (called chelipeds), one of which is larger than the other.

FUN FACTS

- The ghost crab is sometimes called the sand crab.
- These crabs tunnel up to four feet into the sand at a 45° angle, creating 1 to 2 inch-wide holes, which speckle the beach.
- The ghost crab can move at speeds up to 10 miles per hour (4.5 m/s), while making sharp directional changes.
- This creatures uses its sharp 360-degree vision to see flying insects and catch them in mid air.
- The ghost crab has the ability to "deposit feed"—it passes sand through its mouthparts and extracts the nutrients from the algae in the sand.

PHYLUM:	Arthropoda
SUBPHYLUM:	Crustacea
CLASS:	Malacostraca (woodlice, shrimp, lobsters, crabs, etc.)
ORDER:	Decapoda (crabs, shrimp, and relatives)
FAMILY:	Ocypodidae (ghost crabs and fiddler crabs)
GENUS:	*Ocypode* (20 species)
Size:	About 2 in (5 cm)
Diet:	Small crabs, clams, turtle hatchlings, organic matter
Habitat:	Exposed beaches from the tropical and subtropical coasts, including the American Atlantic, through the Mediterranean and Red Sea, to the American Pacific and Indo-Pacific region

GIANT CLAM

GIANT CLAM

CREATED ON DAY 5

DESIGN

The giant clam gets some of its food by filtering the seawater with its siphon. The siphon is fringed with tentacles that attach to food particles in the water. This creature, however, gets most of its nourishment from zooxanthellae, algae that lives within the clam's tissue. This mutualistc relationship between two separate organisms was designed by the Creator to help the clam obtain the great amount of nourishment it needs to survive.

FEATURES

- All giant clams have clear spots on their mantle to let sunlight into their cavity.
- Some giant clams look iridescent because of their blue and purple spots, while others look gold or green.

FUN FACTS

- The giant clam is the heaviest and largest living bivalve mollusk.
- The giant clam cannot completely close its shell once fully grown.
- It starts life as a male, but later becomes hermaphroditic, able to produce both sperm and egg. However, the giant clam does not fertilize itself. It produces sperm and eggs one at a time and releases each into the water to be fertilized by another giant clam.

CLASS:	Bivalvia (bivalves and clams)
ORDER:	Veneroida (clams, cockles, and zebra mussels)
FAMILY:	Tridacnidae (giant clams)
GENUS/SPECIES:	*Tridacna gigas*
Size:	Up to 5 ft (1.5 m) wide; weighs up to 500 lbs (225 kg)
Diet:	Plankton
Habitat:	Sandy beds of reef flats and shallow lagoons in tropical waters of Indo-Pacific Ocean from South China seas, to northern coasts of Australia; and from Nicobar Islands in the west, to Fiji in the east

GIANT OCTOPUS

GIANT OCTOPUS

CREATED ON DAY 5

DESIGN

The octopus can change color to camouflage itself and to reflect its mood. Red indicates that it is annoyed and pale indicates that it is stressed. The octopus changes colors by expanding or contracting the cells that contain the pigment.

FEATURES

- The giant octopus is one of the largest invertebrates. Its arms can reach up to 30 ft (9 m).
- The eight legs of the octopus are covered with sensitive suckers that can distinguish objects.

FUN FACTS

- The octopus will squirt purple "ink" at a supposed predator as a defense mechanism.
- The octopus is considered to be one of the most intelligent sea creatures. This animal can navigate through a maze by trial and error, and then remember the correct way if it needs to navigate the maze again.
- Newly hatched young are the size of a grain of rice.
- The record weight of this species is 600 lbs (272 kg).
- The octopus' sense of touch is very acute.

CLASS:	Cephalopoda (octopuses and squids)
ORDER:	Octopoda (eight-armed)
FAMILY:	Octopodidae
GENUS/SPECIES:	*Enteroctopus dofleini*
Size:	Up to 30 ft (9 m)
Weight:	50–100 lbs (22–45 kg)
Depth:	Down to 2,500 ft (750 m)
Diet:	Small crabs and scallops, snails, fish, turtles, crustaceans
Habitat:	Temperate northwest and northeast Pacific waters

HERMIT CRAB

HERMIT CRAB

CREATED ON DAY 5

DESIGN

Some hermit crabs have an unusual relationship with the sea anemone. The sea anemone has stinging cells that sting or even kill those sea creatures that come into contact with it; however, the hermit crab can carry sea anemones on its shell. And even when the hermit crab changes shells, the sea anemone will often transfer to the new shell. This relationship works for the benefit of both creatures. The sea anemone eats the crab's left-over food particles, and the hermit crab gains protection from predators, as well as some camouflage, from the sea anemone.

FEATURES

- A hermit crab's color varies from red to brown to purple. Some species also have stripes, dots, or other patterns.
- A hermit crab has ten legs. The front two have claws on them, which the crab uses to walk. The rear pair of legs is used to grasp onto the crab's shell.
- The crab's abdomen is uniquely twisted to fit snugly into its shell.

FUN FACTS

- As the hermit crab grows, it must leave its shell and find a larger one. It uses shells that have been abandoned by other sea creatures, hence its nickname, "robber crab."
- The hermit crab's two eyes are located at the ends of short eyestalks.

CLASS:	Malacostraca (crabs, krill, pill bugs, shrimp, and relatives)
ORDER:	Decapoda (crabs, shrimp, and relatives)
FAMILY:	Paguridae (marine hermit crabs)
GENUS/SPECIES:	About 500 species in more than 30 genera
Size:	Varies depending on species
Diet:	Worms, plankton, organic debris
Habitat:	Most waters worldwide

HORSESHOE CRAB

HORSESHOE CRAB

CREATED ON DAY 5

DESIGN

Evolutionists call the horseshoe crab a "living fossil" because fossils of creatures identical to the horseshoe crab have been found and dated to millions of years. During those supposed years of evolution, the horseshoe crab changed very little. This should be no surprise since the horseshoe crab kind was created only a few thousand years ago.

FEATURES

- The soft body of the horseshoe crab is protected by a hard, outer shell.
- The front, smooth part of the shell protects the eyes, legs, pincers, mouth, brain, and heart.
- The middle part of the shell protects the gills and reproductive organs.
- The last part of the shell is the spine that the crab uses to flip itself over if needed.

FUN FACTS

- The horseshoe crab's blood is blue because it is copper-based. Its blood contains a protein that is a key ingredient in a powder used to screen drugs and vaccines for contaminants.
- A horseshoe crab can survive even after losing one-third of its blood.
- It is also said that this creature can go without eating for up to a year.
- The horseshoe crab is not a "true crab" (it's not a crustacean), but is grouped with scorpions, spiders, and extinct trilobites.
- Each spring during the high tides of the new and full moons, thousands of horseshoe crabs descend on the Delaware Bay shoreline to spawn. At the same time, migrating shorebirds descend on Delaware Bay to feed on their eggs, enabling them to have the energy to complete their northward migration.

CLASS:	Merostomata (horseshoe crabs)
ORDER:	Xiphosura
FAMILY:	Limulidae
GENUS/SPECIES:	*Limulus polyphemus*
Size:	Up to 20 in (50 cm)
Diet:	Worms and mollusks
Habitat:	In the shallow waters of the Atlantic coast, from Nova Scotia to the Yucatan and in the Gulf of Mexico

OYSTER

OYSTER

CREATED ON DAY 5

DESIGN

The oyster is a filter-feeder that gets its food by filtering food particles from water with its gills. A healthy oyster can filter up to 1.3 gallons (5 ℓ) of water per hour. This ongoing process by thousands of oysters can rid an area of water pollution, which is extremely beneficial for the water quality, though it is not always good for the oyster.

FEATURES

- An oyster's shell is made up of two valves connected by a muscular hinge. The upper valve is thinner and flat while the lower one thicker and convex. The shell is often highly calcified, with an uneven texture.
- Inside the shell is the soft body of the oyster.
- Oysters grow in piles or clumps known as beds.

FUN FACTS

- The oyster spends most of its life permanently attached to a substrate or lying on the sea floor.
- This creature changes its sex during its life, starting off as a male and usually ending as a female.
- A single female oyster can produce millions of eggs each year.
- Some oysters produce a pearl when foreign material becomes trapped inside the shell. The oyster responds to the irritation by producing nacre, a combination of calcium and protein. The nacre coats the foreign material and over several years produces a pearl.

CLASS:	Bivalvia (bivalves and clams)
SUBCLASS:	Pteriomorpha
ORDER:	Ostreoida (true oysters)
FAMILY:	About 200 species in 10 families
Size:	3–14 in (7.5–35 cm)
Depths:	8–40 ft (2.5–12 m)
Diet:	Plankton, algae
Habitat:	Shallow waters throughout the world's oceans

PURPLE SEA URCHIN

PURPLE SEA URCHIN

CREATED ON DAY 5

DESIGN

The five bony teeth of the sea urchin were given to the original created kind to help it scrape algae (its food) from rocks. The sea urchin also uses its teeth to "carve" away a depression in the rock where it will then settle and grab hold. This feature provides this creature with food and protection.

FEATURES

- The purple sea urchin's color can vary from a deep reddish purple to a light purple.
- The sea urchin has a globe-shaped body, sharp spines, and a hard test, or shell.
- The young purple sea urchin is a shade of green.

FUN FACTS

- The Old English term "urchin" was the name for the spiny hedgehog. The sea urchin resembles a hedgehog in appearance, so it was called "sea urchin."
- The sea urchin does not have a brain.
- The sea urchin's spines can be used in locomotion, defense, and capture of prey.

CLASS:	Echinoidea (heart urchins, sand dollars, and sea urchins)
ORDER:	Echinoida
FAMILY:	Strongylocentrotidae
GENUS/SPECIES:	*Strongylocentrotus purpuratus*
Size:	Average 3.5 in (9 cm)
Diet:	Algae, plankton, and seaweed
Habitat:	Shallow waters off North America's Pacific coast from Alaska to Baja California

QUEEN CONCH

QUEEN CONCH

CREATED ON DAY 5

DESIGN

The conch builds its own shell out of calcium carbonate that it gets from the ocean. How does a conch know that it needs to build a shell, and how does it know how to build its shell? This information was given to the conch kind at creation. Information has to come from a source of intelligence, and that source is the all-knowing Creator God.

FEATURES

- The queen conch, one of the largest marine snails, is best known for its bright pink, orange, or yellow coloring on the inside of the flared lip of its shell.
- The queen conch reaches sexual maturity after three years, when their shells are about 8 in (20 cm) long.

FUN FACTS

- The lip of the conch shell was used by some indigenous people groups to make knives, ax heads, and chisels.
- Abandoned conch shells are often used by many marine creatures, including the cardinal fish and octopuses, as protection from predators.
- The queen conch is also called the pink conch.
- This species has always played a central role in human societies in the Caribbean. For one thing, it is an ideal food source, and it comes in its own cooking pot—its shell!

CLASS:	Gastropoda (gastropods, slugs, and snails)
ORDER:	Neotaenioglossa
FAMILY:	Strombidae (true conchs)
GENUS/SPECIES:	*Strombus gigas*

Size:	6–12 in (15–30.5 cm)
Weight:	Average 4.4 lbs (2 kg)
Diet:	Seagrasses, algae, organic debris
Habitat:	Shallows of semi-tropical and tropical waters of the Caribbean

SCALLOP

SCALLOP

CREATED ON DAY 5

DESIGN

The scallop has an incredibly strong muscle that keeps its shell closed. It also uses this muscle to swim, rapidly opening and closing its shell. When the shell closes, it propels water at great force by means of the velum, which is a fold of the mantle used to direct the flow of water around the hinge. The scallop can sharply change its direction by adjusting its velum.

FEATURES

- The scallop is a bivalve, having two halves to its shell and a soft body.
- It has eyes that can sense changes in light and motion to protect it from predators and help it find food.

FUN FACTS

- The scallop is used in the coat of arms of Winston Churchill's and John Wesley's families.
- Some scallops attach themselves to another structure, but others swim freely.
- Scallops are hermaphroditic—capable of switching sexes.
- A scallop contains two types of meat—the white adductor muscle and the pink or red reproductive glands (called "coral").
- Scallops are considered a delicacy, but generally only the adductor muscle is eaten.

CLASS:	Bivalvia (bivalves and clams)
ORDER:	Ostreoida (true oysters)
FAMILY:	Pectinidae (bivalve mollusks)
GENUS/SPECIES:	About 400 species in more than 30 genera
Size:	Up to 8 in (20 cm) in diameter
Diet:	Plankton
Habitat:	In the sandy and muddy bottoms of the seafloor

SEA ANEMONE

SEA ANEMONE

CREATED ON DAY 5

DESIGN

Some sea anemones have an important symbiotic relationship with algae species. The algae give the sea anemone oxygen and food; and the sea anemone gives the algae protection and food (via waste). Some other sea anemones have a symbiotic relationship with other creatures, such as crabs, shrimp, or clownfish.

FEATURES

- Sea anemones come in a variety of colors and shapes. However, each one is basically a small sac consisting of a column-shaped body that ends in an oral disc. In the middle of this disc is its mouth, which is surrounded by tentacles that are used for defense.
- The sea anemone has nematocysts (stinging cells) on its tentacles, which can be triggered when touched, releasing toxin into its victim.

FUN FACTS

- Most of the time, the sea anemone remains in one place. But if it is continually attacked by predators, it can detach its adhesive foot and swim to a new location.
- The sexes in sea anemones are separate and they can reproduce both sexually and asexually (by a process called budding).

CLASS:	Anthozoa (anemones and corals)
ORDER:	Actiniaria (anemones and sea anemones)
FAMILY:	46 different families
Size:	Less than 0.5 in–6.5 ft (1.3 cm–2 m)
Diet:	Fish, mussels, zooplankton, worms
Habitat:	On rocks, ocean bottoms, and reefs worldwide

SEA CUCUMBER

SEA CUCUMBER

CREATED ON DAY 5

DESIGN

When surprised by a predator, some sea cucumbers can expel their internal organs along with a sticky substance. They then can regrow their innards. Other sea cucumbers can expel all the water in their bodies, becoming hard and small. How would a sea cucumber know to get rid of its insides to escape a predator? This information was programmed into its DNA by its Creator.

FEATURES

- The sea cucumber is a long, cylindrical invertebrate. It doesn't have arms; instead it has five double rows of tube feet along the length of its body.
- The sea cucumber also has spines on its skin.
- Most are black, green, or brown.
- It has ten tentacles surrounding its mouth.

FUN FACTS

- The largest sea cucumber measured 6.5 ft (2 m) long.
- The sea cucumber does not have a brain.
- Sea cucumbers are considered a delicacy in Far Eastern countries such as Malaysia, China, Japan, Korea, and Indonesia.

CLASS:	Holothuroidea (sea cucumbers)
ORDER:	Six different orders
FAMILY:	23 different families
GENUS/SPECIES:	Over 1,100 species
Size:	Most up to 16 in (40 cm)
Diet:	Plankton, decaying organic matter
Habitat:	Found on seafloors worldwide in both tropical waters and cold trenches

SEA SLUG

SEA SLUG

CREATED ON DAY 5

DESIGN

Sea slugs have a number of defense mechanisms. Some of them have a nasty taste, others are able to camouflage themselves, and others are able to eat sea anemones and store their stinging cells in their body wall to ward off predators. The information for these defense mechanisms was given to these creatures by their Creator.

FEATURES

- Most sea slugs are brightly colored, which may warn potential predators to stay away.
- Sea slugs are soft-bodied snails that have no shell or plates to protect them.
- Sea slugs have tentacles that are sensitive to touch, smell, and taste.

FUN FACTS

- Sea slugs are also called nudibranchs.
- Nudibranchs are simultaneous hermaphrodites, which means that they possess both male and female sex organs at the same time. This design increases the probability of finding a mate, since every mature individual of the same species is a potential partner.
- Many nudibranchs have numerous feathery extensions on various parts of their bodies. These structures provide ample surface area for respiratory exchange.

CLASS:	Gastropoda
ORDER:	Opisthobranchia
SUBORDER:	Nudibranchia
GENUS/SPECIES:	More than 3,000 species
Size:	Varies greatly; most between 0.2–24 in (0.4–60 cm)
Diet:	Seaweed, sponges, coral
Habitat:	Found at all depths worldwide

SEA STAR

SEA STAR

CREATED ON DAY 5

DESIGN

To feed on hard-shelled prey like a clam, the sea star firmly grasps it with its arms until the clam slightly opens its shell. The sea star then pushes its stomach out of its mouth and into the clam and begins to digest its insides. When the clam is digested, the sea star pulls its stomach back inside its own body. The information for such a feeding habit was given to the sea star by its all-knowing Creator.

FEATURES

- The sea star usually has five sections or arms, or multiples of 5, 10, 20, or even 40 arms.
- The top half of its body is covered by a hard, spiny covering, with small pincers. Its underside is soft and fleshy, with dozens of tube feet on its arms, which function in movement and feeding.

FUN FACTS

- Sea stars are also known as starfish, but they are not fish at all.
- A sea star can regrow arms that are lost, and if cut in half, some sea stars can grow into two separate creatures.
- The fastest sea star moves at 360 ft per hour (110 m/h)—that's only slightly faster than a snail.

CLASS:	Asteroidea
ORDER:	Seven orders
FAMILY:	Varies depending on order
GENUS/SPECIES:	Over 1,800 different species
Size:	Varies greatly depending on species
Diet:	Barnacles, chitons, snails, urchins, limpets, sponges, and sea anemones
Habitat:	Worldwide in all of earth's oceans

SPANISH DANCER

SPANISH DANCER

CREATED ON DAY 5

DESIGN

Part of this creature's defense mechanism is its bright coloring. Also, when laying its eggs, the female Spanish dancer deposits a toxin with them, which keeps predators from eating the undeveloped Spanish dancers. The information for these habits was given to this creature by its Creator.

FEATURES

- The Spanish dancer's flattened body is brightly colored in shades of red, pink, or orange.
- Some are a solid color and some are patterned, depending on the location.
- This is the only nudibranch family that has six gills.

FUN FACTS

- This creature gets its name from the appearance of its swimming motion. It resembles the flaring skirt of a Spanish dancer.
- The male Spanish dancer enters dance competitions to win its mate.
- This creature is one of the most colorful in the world.
- This species was first described in the Red Sea, where its solid red form is found.

CLASS:	Gastropoda
ORDER:	Nudibranchia
FAMILY:	Hexabranchidae
GENUS/SPECIES:	*Hexabranchus sanguineus*
Size:	Up to 1.5 ft (0.45 m)
Diet:	Sponges
Habitat:	Shallow waters of tropical Indian Ocean and western Pacific, on coasts and reefs

SPONGE

SPONGE

CREATED ON DAY 5

DESIGN

God designed the sponge with the ability to draw water into its body through tiny holes. It then filters the water for food and oxygen before pushing the water out again. Sponges pump remarkable amounts of water. Many sponges produce toxic chemicals that keep predators from eating them.

FEATURES

- The sponge's shape comes from a skeleton that is made up of tiny spicules of hard minerals located throughout its body.
- Sponges come in a variety of shapes such as tubes, spheres, and threads.

FUN FACTS

- A sponge has no organs, just specialized cells. They represent the simplest of animals.
- A sponge digests its food within individual cells.
- With no true tissues, the sponge lacks muscles, nerves, and internal organs.
- Sponges have been found as deep as 28,000 ft (8,500 m).
- New species of sponges are constantly being discovered.

CLASS:	Three classes: Hexactinellida (glass sponges); Calcarea; and Demospongiae
ORDER:	Varies depending on class
FAMILY:	Varies depending on class
GENUS/SPECIES:	More than 5,000 species
Size:	Varies greatly
Diet:	Plankton
Habitat:	Coral reefs, rock reefs, and sunken ships in the western Pacific Ocean

SQUID

CREATED ON DAY 5

DESIGN

The squid, like other cephalopods, has design features for jet propulsion under water. It expands its mantle cavity and sucks water into its body, then relaxes its muscles, which in turn forces the water out through its siphon. The direction of the siphon can be changed in order to control the direction of travel.

FEATURES

- The squid has two fins, a mantle, and a head that bears eight arms and two tentacles, each covered with suckers, which are armed with hooks or sucker rings.
- The mouth of the squid is equipped with a sharp horny beak made of chitin.

FUN FACTS

- The giant squid is one of the largest invertebrates ever to exist in the world's oceans. It has one of the largest eyes of any animal in the world—over 1 ft (30 cm) in diameter.
- In 2003, a large specimen of the colossal squid was discovered. It is thought to be able to grow to 46 ft (14 m), making it the largest invertebrate.
- The skin of the squid is covered in chromatophores, which enable the squid to change color to suit its surroundings.
- The squid has three hearts.
- It has the ability to release a cloud of dark ink into the water when disturbed. This forms a "smoke screen," which camouflages its escape.

CLASS:	Cephalopoda (octopuses and squids)
ORDER:	Teuthida (squids)
FAMILY:	29 families in two suborders
SPECIES:	About 500 species
Size:	From 2 in (5 cm) to up to 46 ft (14 m), including tentacles; average 24 in (60 cm)
Diet:	Fish, crustaceans, and smaller squids
Habitat:	All oceans worldwide

WHELK

WHELK

CREATED ON DAY 5

DESIGN

The whelk uses its radula (a tongue-like feature with rows of teeth) to bore a hole into the shell of its prey to reach the protected flesh. It then sucks out the flesh.

FEATURES

- A whelk is generally light gray to tan, often having brown and white streaks.
- The thick-lipped, spiral shell has an uneven surface with many protrusions. The shell coils in a right-hand direction and has a long siphonal canal.
- The shape of the whelk depends on the waves that impact the creature.
- The whelk has a large, muscular foot with which it holds its victim.

FUN FACTS

- The color of the whelk depends on the foods that it eats.
- Whelk egg masses, resembling clumps of puffed rice, are commonly found on beaches in early summer.
- The whelk is one of the most common rocky-shore gastropods in temperate regions.

CLASS:	Gastropoda (gastropods, slugs, and snails)
ORDER:	Sorbeoconcha
FAMILY:	Muricidae, Buccinidae, and Melongenidae
SPECIES:	About 15 species
Size:	From 1 in (2.5 cm) up to 16 in (41 cm)
Depth:	Up to 160 ft (48 m)
Diet:	Oysters, clams, mussels, and scallops
Habitat:	Rocky shores of northwestern and northeastern Atlantic coasts

ALBATROSS

ALBATROSS

CREATED ON DAY 5

DESIGN

With its large wings, the albatross uses wind currents to aid in extended flights. This bird utilizes a unique method of flight called dynamic soaring, usually only flapping its wings on takeoff and landing. In order to take off, the albatross takes a running start with outstretched wings. In calm weather, this bird floats in the ocean.

FEATURES

- The albatross is one of the largest flying birds with wings that are long and narrow.
- Depending on the species, the body is predominately white or light to dark gray.
- The bill is covered in plates and along the sides are two tubes, which are actually long nostrils.

FUN FACTS

- The wandering and royal albatrosses have the largest wingspan of any bird, up to 11 ft (3.4 m) from tip to tip.
- Albatrosses generally mate for life. This mate is usually selected after courtship "dances," which include bill-circling, sky-pointing, and flank-touching.
- The albatross is among the most oceanic of all seabirds, and it seldom approaches land except to breed.
- Each year an albatross can cover a distance equivalent to flying around the earth at the equator three times.
- The heart of the wandering albatross actually beats slower during flight than when sitting on the sea.

CLASS:	Aves (birds)
ORDER:	Procellariiformes (tube-nosed seabirds)
FAMILY:	Diomedeidae (albatrosses)
GENUS/SPECIES:	Four genera with about 20 species
Size:	2–4 ft (0.6– 1.2 m); wingspan up to 11 ft (3.4 m)
Weight:	10–20 lbs (4.5–9 kg)
Diet:	Fish, crustaceans, octopuses, and squid
Habitat:	Southern hemisphere from Antarctica to Australia, South Africa, and South America; North Pacific, from Hawaii To Japan, California, and Alaska

ANHINGA

ANHINGA

CREATED ON DAY 5

DESIGN

The anhinga's neck, bill, and feet all help it catch prey. The neck can be bent back in an S-shape, and the powerful neck muscles, when tightened, enable the bird to thrust its head forward with great force, like a harpoon. The bill is straight, sharp, and pointed, in the form of a dagger.

FEATURES

- The anhinga has a small head and a long, slender neck. It uses its long and serrated bill to spear fish. Its webbed feet help it swim.
- Males are black with greenish irridescence and adult females have a buffy neck and breast. Both sexes have silvery-white spots and streaks on wings and upper back.

FUN FACTS

- The anhinga sheds its flight feathers all at once, which makes it unable to fly for a while. During this time, it is totally silent so it doesn't reveal its location.
- The anhinga is also called water turkey, snake bird, or darter.
- It swims with only its head held out of the water.
- The anhinga's feathers are not waterproof, so after spending some time in the water fishing, it comes out, perches on a rock or tree limb, and spreads its feathers to dry and warm in the sun.

CLASS:	Aves (birds)
ORDER:	Pelecaniformes (pelicans, tropicbirds, cormorants, and relatives)
FAMILY:	Anhingidae (anhingas and darters)
GENUS/SPECIES:	*Anhinga anhinga*
Size:	Body 3.3 ft (1 m); wingspan 4 ft (1.2 m)
Weight:	Average 3 lbs (1.4 kg)
Diet:	Primarily fish
Habitat:	Swamps, coastal bays, lakes, marshes, and lagoons with shrub and tree-covered lands in the southeast U.S., central America, and eastern South America

ARCTIC TERN

ARCTIC TERN

CREATED ON DAY 5

DESIGN

The Arctic tern, with its streamlined body and long, pointed wings, is uniquely designed for its long, yearly flight. It also has very keen eyesight. The Arctic tern locates schools of fish in shallow water and seizes its prey at the water's surface while in flight. It can also locate insects on land and catch them while in flight. These abilities were given to the Arctic tern by its Creator.

FEATURES

- The Arctic tern has a white body with a black cap on its head, gray upper wings, back, and underparts, and a deeply forked white tail.
- In the spring, the bill is a deep red.
- The legs of the Arctic tern are extremely short.

FUN FACTS

- The female tern gets a mate by chasing him through the air. The male then courts her by giving her a fish.
- This bird hovers over the water and then dives to capture its prey.
- The Arctic tern has the second longest regular migration of any known animal, traveling from the Arctic to the Antarctic and back again—about 12,000 miles (19,000 km) each year.
- The tern's polar migration allows it to experience two summers per year and to see more daylight than any other animal on earth.

CLASS: Aves (birds)
ORDER: Charadriiformes (shorebirds and relatives)
FAMILY: Sternidae (terns)
GENUS/SPECIES: *Sterna paradisaea*

Size: 14–17 in (36–43 cm); wingspan 29–33 in (74–84 cm)
Diet: Mostly small fish, crustaceans, and insects
Habitat: Nests long seacoasts, interior lakes, and marshes north of the Arctic Circle worldwide; winters in sub-Antarctic and Antarctic waters

ATLANTIC PUFFIN

ATLANTIC PUFFIN

CREATED ON DAY 5

DESIGN

The puffin has a large triangular bill, which is very efficient at catching and holding small fish. It also has a special gland that produces oil, with which it waterproofs its feathers. A puffins can dive as deep as 100 ft (30 m) into the ocean for fish. While underwater it uses its small wings as propellers and its webbed feet like paddles.

FEATURES

- All three species of puffins stand upright and have black and white head and body plumage. They also have brightly-colored bills, mostly yellow and orange.
- The legs and feet are orange.

FUN FACTS

- The Atlantic puffin can fly at speeds up to 50 mph (80 km/h). It achieves this amazing speed by beating its wings rapidly, up to 400 beats per minute.
- The outer part of the puffin's bill sheds after mating season.
- The large colorful bill of the puffin caused early sailors to give them the nickname "sea parrot."
- The Atlantic puffin spends the winter out at sea.

CLASS:	Aves (birds)
ORDER:	Charadriiformes (shorebirds and relatives)
FAMILY:	Alcidae (auks)
GENUS/SPECIES:	*Fratercula arctica*
Size:	12–14 in (30–36 cm)
Weight:	About 1 lb (0.5 kg)
Diet:	Small fish, mollusks, and crustaceans
Habitat:	Greenland and Northern Canada, Gulf of St. Lawrence, Nova Scotia, Iceland, Northern Scandinavia, Northern Russia, Ireland, and NW coast of France

COMMON MURRE

COMMON MURRE

CREATED ON DAY 5

DESIGN

The common murre dives after its food, often to depths of 100 ft (30 m). However, it has been recorded reaching a depth of 550 ft (168 m). Its strong wings propel it through the water and enable it to catch its prey. The common murre does not build a nest. The female lays a single egg on a bare rock ledge, and both parents take turns incubating it. The egg is so pointed on one end that it rolls in a circle if it is pushed. That's a great design to keep the egg from rolling off the rocky ledge.

FEATURES

- The common murre is sometimes confused with penguins. It resembles the penguin somewhat in shading with a white underbelly and dark head, neck, back, wings, and tail, and also in its upward posture.

FUN FACTS

- The common murre spends the majority of its life at sea, only coming ashore to breed.
- The eggs of the common murre vary in color, from white to light green, blue, or brown. The coloring may help the parents recognize their eggs.
- Some of the sounds this bird makes include purrs, growls, and croaks.
- The lining of the common murre's mouth is yellow.
- Its winter distribution is largely determined by the concentration of schooling fish, its prey.

CLASS: Aves (birds)
ORDER: Charadriiformes (shorebirds and relatives)
FAMILY: Alcidae (auks)
GENUS/SPECIES: *Uria aalge*

Size: 15–17 in (38–43 cm); wingspan between 25–28 in (64–71 cm)
Diet: Mainly fish; but also shrimp, mollusks, and squid
Habitat: Coasts of western Alaska to central California; coasts of Labrador to Nova Scotia; during the winter, mostly offshore

DOUBLE-CRESTED CORMORANT

DOUBLE-CRESTED CORMORANT

CREATED ON DAY 5

DESIGN

The double-crested cormorant is designed with a hook-like tip on its bill, which helps it capture its prey underwater. The cormorant, like the anhinga, doesn't have oil glands to properly waterproof its feathers. It must come ashore to dry out its feathers so it can fly again.

FEATURES

- The double-crested cormorant's feathers are dark brown or black with a greenish tint. It has a lean body, a long neck, and somewhat short wings. During the breeding season, the double-crested cormorant has blue eyelids, orange on its throat sacs, and two black crests.

FUN FACTS

- The bright colors of the double-crested cormorant are used to attract a mate during the breeding season. But after the mating season is over, the crests and blue eyelids are lost, and the orange coloring becomes yellow.

CLASS:	Aves (birds)
ORDER:	Pelecaniformes (pelicans, tropicbirds, cormorants, and relatives)
FAMILY:	Phalacrocoracidae (cormorants)
GENUS/SPECIES:	*Phalacrocorax auritus*
Size:	2–3 ft (0.6–1 m); wingspan up to 52 in (132 cm)
Weight:	2.5–5.5 lbs (1.1–2.5 kg)
Diet:	Primarily fish; sometimes crustaceans, insects, and amphibians
Habitat:	North America, as far north as southern Alaska, and as far south as Mexico

EMPEROR PENGUIN

EMPEROR PENGUIN

CREATED ON DAY 5

DESIGN

Baby penguins hatch at just the right time. During the winter months when the young hatch, the ocean is farthest away from the penguins. By the time the young are ready to enter the ocean, the ice pack has melted, bringing the water's edge closest to them. To keep warm against the harsh Antarctic wind and subzero temperatures while incubating its egg, the male penguin huddles with other males in a huge circle. They take turns moving from the outer, colder area to the inner, warmer area. This instinct is part of God's protection for this species.

FEATURES

- The emperor penguin is the largest of the penguin species.
- An orange-yellow band extends from behind the eyes of the emperor penguin downward to the neck and chest area. There is also orange coloring on its lower beak.
- It is easily recognized with its jet black head, grayish-black wings and back, and white belly.
- All penguins are flightless on land, but do "fly" very well under water.

FUN FACTS

- The male is responsible for incubating the egg. He carries it on his feet and protects it in his brood pouch while the female leaves to hunt for food.
- While the female is gone, the male goes without food for nearly 2 months.
- The emporer penguin can dive to a depth of more than 1,500 ft (450 m).

CLASS:	Aves (birds)
ORDER:	Sphenisciformes (penguins)
FAMILY:	Spheniscidae (penguins)
GENUS/SPECIES:	*Aptenodytes forsteri*
Size:	Average almost 4 ft (1.2 m)
Weight:	40–100 lbs (18–46 kg)
Diet:	Mainly fish, also krill and cephalopods
Habitat:	In Antarctic waters; nests on ice floes or Antarctic mainland

FLAMINGO

FLAMINGO

CREATED ON DAY 5

DESIGN

The flamingo sucks water and mud into its beak with its unique tongue and then pumps the water out the sides of its mouth. Small creatures are captured in the flamingo's filtering system of tiny plates. Flamingos feed in a manner similar to that of baleen whales.

FEATURES

- The flamingo is known for its bright pink feathers and uniquely downcurved black-tipped bill, which is adapted to filter feeding.
- The flamingo is quite unmistakable, with its remarkably long legs and neck.

FUN FACTS

- The flamingo's pink color comes from the food that it eats.
- The flamingo uses different displays, including head-flagging, wing saluting, twist-preening, and marching.
- All five species of flamingos have black flight feathers.
- Flamingos can fly up to 35 mph (60 km/h).
- Flocks tend to fly in lines or in V-formation, like geese and cranes.

CLASS:	Aves (birds)
ORDER:	Phoenicopteriformes (flamingos)
FAMILY:	Phoenicopteridae (flamingos)
GENUS/SPECIES:	*Phoenicopterus* (six species)
Size:	About 3–5 ft (1–1.6 m) tall; wingspan 3–5 ft (1–1.6 m)
Weight:	Between 3 and 9 lbs (1.4–4 kg)
Diet:	Algae, shrimp, and other small aquatic creatures
Habitat:	Africa, Asia, the Americas, and Europe in shallow lakes or lagoons

GLAUCOUS-WINGED GULL

GLAUCOUS-WINGED GULL

CREATED ON DAY 5

DESIGN

The glaucous-winged gull eats mollusks that have hard outer shells by dropping them onto coastal rocks from the air to break them open. How does the gull know to do this to get to the food inside the shell? The Creator either gave the gulls the ability to learn this behavior, or it was programmed into the gull from the beginning.

FEATURES

- The adult glaucous-winged gull has pale gray wings and back, a white body, and pink legs. Its bill is yellow with a red spot. The skin around the eyes is a pink color.
- The head and neck of non-breeding adults is streaked with brownish-gray.

FUN FACTS

- Some of the calls of the glaucous-winged gull sound like cries, chuckles, and hisses.
- The adult gull regurgitates food for its young.
- This bird often spends a lot of time on land eating the garbage from the docks.
- In addition to mollusks, this species of gull feeds on salmon roe (eggs) and the remains of dead or dying fish killed by bears during spawning runs.

CLASS:	Aves (birds)
ORDER:	Charadriiformes (shorebirds and relatives)
FAMILY:	Laridae (gulls and terns)
GENUS/SPECIES:	*Larus glaucescens*
Size:	2–2.3 ft (0.6–0.7 m); wingspan 4.5 ft (1.4 m)
Diet:	Includes carrion, fish, invertebrates, eggs, and small mammals
Habitat:	Primarily along the coasts of the northern Pacific Ocean, from Alaska and the Aleutian Islands to northern Washington state; winters as far as Baja, California and the Hawaiian Islands

GREAT WHITE PELICAN

GREAT WHITE PELICAN

CREATED ON DAY 5

DESIGN

The great white pelican lives, feeds, breeds, flies, and migrates in large flocks. When feeding, the flock surrounds schools of fish and forces them into shallow water, making the fish an easy catch. However, this feeding method was not part of the original created kind's habit until after the Fall of man.

FEATURES

- The great white pelican has white feathers with black wing tips.
- Its bill is yellow, blue, and pink with a small pink hook on the tip and a distinctive, elastic yellow pouch underneath.
- The female is slightly smaller than the male.

FUN FACTS

- The pelican's bill can reach over 18 in (45 cm).
- The majority of the great white pelican's day is spent loafing around on sandbars and small islands.
- The pelican eats a captured fish whole.
- This bird is one of the largest flying birds in the world.
- It breeds in trees, which may be killed by repeated nesting. Each nesting colony contains 20–500 pairs of pelicans.
- Chicks hatch naked but soon grow white down feathers. It takes about 84 days for the chick to fledge (leave the nest).

CLASS:	Aves (birds)
ORDER:	Pelecaniformes (pelicans, tropicbirds, cormorants, and relatives)
FAMILY:	Pelecanidae (pelicans)
GENUS/SPECIES:	*Pelecanus onocrotalus*
Size:	Male 6 ft (1.8 m); female 4.5 ft (1.4 m); average wingspan 10 ft (3 m)
Diet:	Mainly fish
Habitat:	Eastern Europe to Western Mongolia; Migrates to Northeast Africa and Iraq to Northern India

MANDARIN DUCK

MANDARIN DUCK

CREATED ON DAY 5

DESIGN

This bird is not hunted for food because it has a bad taste. This feature may have been part of its Creator's design to help protect it from predators after the Fall.

FEATURES

- The multi-colored mandarin duck has gray, green, black, and brown upperparts with white underneath. It has orange and cream feathers with a broad patch of white around its eyes. It also has a pair of orange-gold feathers that are raised vertically along its back and a red beak with a light tip.
- The female mandarin duck is more muted and gray in appearance with a white band around its eyes, and a narrow white line behind her eyes. Her belly is whitish.

FUN FACTS

- The mandarin duck lays its eggs high in a tree cavity, usually over water, sometimes up to 30 ft (9 m) above the ground.
- After the chicks hatch, the mother will call to them from the ground, and they will jump to the ground in order to search for food. Don't worry, the great fall does not seem to hurt the chicks.
- This species' numbers are declining due to habitat destruction and exportation in vast numbers over many years.

CLASS:	Aves (birds)
ORDER:	Anseriformes (waterfowl)
FAMILY:	Anatidae (ducks, geese, and swans)
GENUS/SPECIES:	*Aix galericulata*
Size:	About 8–10 in (20–25.4 cm)
Weight:	Male 1.5 lbs (0.7 kg); female 2.5 lbs (1.1 kg)
Diet:	Plants and seeds, as well as insects, small fish, and land snails
Habitat:	Breeds in Siberia, China, and Japan; winters in the forests of southern China and Japan; some are also found in England, where they were introduced

ROSEATE SPOONBILL

ROSEATE SPOONBILL

CREATED ON DAY 5

DESIGN

The roseate spoonbill feeds by wading slowly through the water, sweeping its long bill from side to side, capturing insects, minnows, plants, and small crustaceans.

FEATURES

- The roseate spoonbill has a greenish unfeathered head, white neck and back, pink wings and underparts, and red legs and eyes. Feathers on its shoulders can be red during breeding.
- Its most distinctive feature is its gray spoon-shaped bill, which is very long.

FUN FACTS

- The roseate spoonbill makes strange, guttural noises while it eats.
- The roseate spoonbill's pink coloration comes from the carotenoid pigments contained in the organisms in its diet.
- It flies in diagonal formation with other spoonbills.
- In the 1800s, roseate spoonbills were nearly hunted to extinction because their beautiful pink feathers were highly prized for women's hats and fans.

CLASS:	Aves (birds)
ORDER:	Ciconiiformes (storks, herons, and relatives)
FAMILY:	Threskiornithidae (ibises and spoonbills)
GENUS/SPECIES:	*Ajaia ajaja*
Size:	Average 2.5 ft (0.8 m)
Diet:	Mainly aquatic insects, also crayfish, shrimp, fish, and occasionally mollusks and plant matter
Habitat:	Inland wetlands with fresh or brackish water from Florida and the Gulf Coast of Texas to Central and South America

BELUGA WHALE

BELUGA WHALE

CREATED ON DAY 5

DESIGN

About fifty percent of the beluga whale's weight is fat, and its blubber is about 4 in (10 cm) thick. These features are possibly adaptations of the original created kind as it adjusted to the colder waters of the Arctic region. The area's climate would have dramatically changed after the Ice Age that followed the global Flood.

FEATURES

- The beluga whale is known for its milky white skin. Young are gray or pinkish brown at birth but fade to white as they grow.
- The beluga whale does not have a dorsal fin. This unique design feature allows it to swim near the water's surface under the ice.
- Its white color acts to camouflage it in its icy environment.
- Males are larger than females.

FUN FACTS

- The beluga whale is also called the white whale or sea canary, due to its vocalizations.
- Its melon (the fatty lump of tissue on its forhead) is very large and is used in echolocation. The beluga is able to change the shape of the melon by blowing air around its sinuses.
- Belugas are very social animals and congregate in pods (social groups) of 2–25 whales. During migration several pods may join together, forming a group of more than 1,000 animals.
- Mating occurs in the spring and young are born in the summer after a gestation period of 14 months.

CLASS:	Mammalia (mammals)
ORDER:	Cetacea (dolphins, porpoises, and whales)
FAMILY:	Monodontidae (beluga and narwhal)
GENUS/SPECIES:	*Delphinapterus leucas*
Size:	16 ft (5 m)
Weight:	Average 2,975–3,300 lbs (1,350–1,500 kg)
Diet:	Octopus, squid, crabs, shrimp, clams, and fish
Habitat:	Arctic and sub-Arctic coastal waters of Canada, Alaska, Greenland, Norway, and Russia

BOTTLENOSE DOLPHIN

BOTTLENOSE DOLPHIN

CREATED ON DAY 5

DESIGN

A dolphin's skin is actually composed of three layers: the epidermis, dermis, and hypodermis (blubber layer). Its core temperature is kept warm by this layer of blubber. The skin contains microdermal ridges, which trap water molecules at the surface of the skin, allowing the dolphin to swim with less resistance, since a liquid moves more easily past another liquid than past a solid. What a wonderful provision by the dolphin's Creator.

FEATURES

- A bottlenose dolphin's color varies from a dark gray near its dorsal fin to a light gray on its sides to an almost white on its belly.
- The name "bottlenose" comes from this dolphin's elongated upper and lower jaws that form what is called the "rostrum."

FUN FACTS

- To establish dominance over one another, male dolphins will butt heads.
- The dolphin locates its food by using a form of echolocation.
- It communicates through squeaks, whistles, and body movement.
- The up and down motion of the dolphin's tail fluke helps bring its head up to the surface so it can breathe through the blowhole on top of its head.
- The outer surface of the dolphin's skin is replaced about every two to four hours.
- A dolphin can hold its breath up to 20 minutes.
- Bottlenose dolphins are the most common cetacean in captivity. They were first successfully held captive in 1914.

CLASS:	Mammalia (mammals)
ORDER:	Cetacea (dolphins, porpoises, and whales)
FAMILY:	Delphinidae (dolphins, killer whales, pilot whales, and relatives)
GENUS/SPECIES:	*Tursiops truncates* (common bottlenose dolphin); *T. aduncus* (Indo-Pacific bottlenose dolphin); other subspecies
Size:	6–13 ft (1.8–4 m)
Weight:	330–650 lbs (150–295 kg)
Diet:	Fish, squid, and crustaceans

CALIFORNIA SEA LION

CALIFORNIA SEA LION

CREATED ON DAY 5

DESIGN

The sea lion uses a system of echolocation to navigate while under water and to find food. A mother leaves her newborn pup while she goes hunting. To relocate each other, they "bark" until they find one other. The mother then smells the pup to completely identify it as her own. While underwater, the sea lion can open its mouth to capture prey without swallowing water because of special muscles that close off the nostrils, larynx, and esophagus.

FEATURES

- The sea lion has a brownish coat with lighter coloring on its belly and sides.
- It has front flippers as well as two back flippers. These flippers are all coated with short, dark stubble.
- The sea lion has tiny external ear flaps.

FUN FACTS

- A sea lion can be easily trained, making it a great attraction at circuses and aquariums.
- These animals have been known to "adopt" an abandoned pup.
- The sea lion can rotate its hind flippers underneath its body to help it walk on land.
- The sea lion swims using a sweeping motion of its two large front flippers, using the hind flippers to steer.
- It can sleep while floating in water.

CLASS:	Mammalia (mammals)
ORDER:	Carnivora (meat-eating)
SUBORDER:	Pinnipedia (fin-footed)
FAMILY:	Otariidae (eared seals)
GENUS/SPECIES:	*Zalophus californianus*
Size:	Almost 8 ft (2.4 m)
Weight:	Up to 860 lbs (390 kg)
Diet:	Fish and mollusks
Habitat:	Marine, in three temperate areas (Westcoast of North America, Galapagos Islands, and southern Sea of Japan)

HARBOR SEAL

HARBOR SEAL

CREATED ON DAY 5

DESIGN

Like other marine mammals, the harbor seal has a lower heart rate than land-dwelling mammals. Its body also has the ability to "transfer" blood supply to its vital organs when diving. It also has more blood than a land-dwelling mammal of comparable size, which allows it to retain more oxygen. These features are probably adaptations of the original created kind since the temperatures on land and in the ocean drastically changed following the global Flood and the Ice Age.

FEATURES

- The harbor seal is covered by a coat of short, thick hairs. These hairs are white to black.
- Its back is covered with darker spots or rings.
- It also has four webbed flippers that help it move through the water. The hind flippers move from side to side propelling it forward in the water and the front flippers are used for steering.

FUN FACTS

- This seal is also known as the common seal.
- The harbor seal can dive to depths exceeding 600 ft (185 m) and can remain submerged for over 20 minutes.
- The harbor seal cannot walk on all four limbs like a sea lion. It moves awkwardly on land, but is well-suited for the water environment.
- One way to tell a seal from a sea lion is that the seal has no visible ear flaps.

CLASS:	Mammalia (mammal)
ORDER:	Carnivora (meat-eating)
SUBORDER:	Pinnipedia (fin-footed)
FAMILY:	Phocidae (true seals)
GENUS/SPECIES:	*Phoca vitulina*; four or five subspecies
Size:	6.5 ft (2 m)
Weight:	110–375 lbs (50–170 kg); males larger than females
Diet:	Squid, crustaceans, mollusks, and a variety of fish
Habitat:	Coastal waters of the northern Atlantic and Pacific Oceans; also in the Baltic Sea and North Sea

KILLER WHALE

KILLER WHALE

CREATED ON DAY 5

DESIGN

Killer whales live in groups called pods. Sometimes the members of the pod will hunt together, surrounding large prey and forcing it into a smaller area before attacking. This hunting technique was likely not part of the original whale kind at creation since all animals were vegetarian until after the Fall of man.

FEATURES

- The killer whale is easily recognized by its black body, white lower jaw and belly, and white patch directly behind the eye.
- Killer whales are the largest member of the dolphin family.
- The most conspicuous external feature of this species is its tall dorsal fin, which can be seen from a great distance.

FUN FACTS

- A newborn killer whale calf averages 8 ft (2.4 m) in length and weighs 300–400 lbs (135–180 kg).
- The largest male killer whale known weighed 22,000 lbs (10,000 kg).
- The killer whale is the fastest swimming mammal, attaining speeds up to 30 mph (48 km/h).
- Killer whales survive long periods of time in captivity, and they are easily trained to perform awe-inspiring feats.

CLASS:	Mammalia (mammals)
ORDER:	Cetacea (dolphins, porpoises, and whales)
FAMILY:	Delphinidae (dolphins, killer whales, pilot whales, and relatives)
GENUS/SPECIES:	*Orcinus orca*
Size:	Male 19–30 ft (5.8–9.5 m); female 16–22 ft (4.9–7 m)
Weight:	Male 8,000–16,000 lbs (3,600–7,300 kg); female 3,000–8,000 lbs (1,400–3,600 kg)
Diet:	Fish, marine mammals, sea turtles, and birds
Habitat:	Worldwide distribution, but more common in the colder regions of the Arctic and Antarctic

MANATEE

MANATEE

CREATED ON DAY 5

DESIGN

The manatee has an incredible immune system. It is able to heal after great injury, even injuries caused by boats. The manatee has a very sensitive pattern of whiskers on its snout for sensing its food supply in the dark, murky waters where it sometimes frequents.

FEATURES

- The manatee is a large, gray aquatic mammal with a body that tapers to a flat, paddle-shaped tail or fluke. It has two forelimbs or flippers, each with three to four nails, and no hind limbs. Its head and face are wrinkled with whiskers on the snout.
- The up and down motion of its tail helps arch the manatee's back and raise its nostrils to the surface for breathing.

FUN FACTS

- The manatee is often referred to as the sea cow.
- The manatee has no incisors. It only has molars, which are used for grinding vegetation. These molars are sometimes called "marching teeth" because they move forward, are worn down, and are continually being replaced.
- A manatee can weigh between 60 and 70 lbs (27–32 kg) at birth.
- The manatee is the largest of all freshwater animals.
- Manatees communicate with a wide range of sounds, especially between cows and their calves.
- The manatee is a vegetarian and can eat 10-15% of its body weight in food per day.

CLASS:	Mammalia (mammal)
ORDER:	Sirenia (mammals living in water)
FAMILY:	Trichechidae (manatees)
GENUS/SPECIES:	*Trichechus inunguis* (Amazonian); *T. senegalensis* (West African), and *T. manatus* (West Indian)
Size:	Average 10 ft (3 m)
Weight:	900–1,200 lbs (410–545 kg)
Diet:	Plants
Habitat:	Aquatic, in sub-tropical and tropical areas

SEA OTTER

SEA OTTER

CREATED ON DAY 5

DESIGN

The sea otter is one of the few animals known to use tools. It uses small rocks or other objects to pry prey from rocks and to hammer or pry open its food. The sea otter can dive up to 330 ft (100 m) when foraging for food. God gave the sea otter the thickest fur in the animal kingdom. Unlike other marine mammals, the sea otter does not have a layer of blubber (fat) to help keep it warm.

FEATURES

- When the sea otter is underwater, its ears and nostrils close.
- The sea otter has webbed hind feet which are perfect for swimming; its forefeet are smaller with semi-retractable claws.

FUN FACTS

- A sea otter's fur contains an estimated 650,000 hairs per square inch. Air is trapped between the hairs, keeping the animal dry.
- Since a sea otter must generate a large amount of heat to maintain its body temperature, it must eat about 20 lbs (9 kg) of food a day. Abalone is its favorite food.
- The sea otter sleeps and rests on its back, usually anchored in a kelp (seaweed) bed.
- It sleeps at sea, sometimes joining hundreds of others in resting areas called rafts.
- Sea otters give birth in the ocean.

CLASS:	Mammalia (mammal)
ORDER:	Carnivora (meat-eating)
SUBORDER:	Pinnipedia (fin-footed)
FAMILY:	Mustelidae (sub-family Lutrinae)
GENUS/SPECIES:	*Enhydra lutris*
Size:	4–5 ft (1.2–1.5 m)
Weight:	Average between 64 and 85 lbs (29–39 kg)
Diet:	Clams, crabs, fish, and octopuses
Habitat:	Pacific coastal and estuarine areas of North America and Asia

WALRUS

WALRUS

CREATED ON DAY 5

DESIGN

The thick, wrinkled skin acts as a protective barrier for the walrus when it fights with other walruses and when it is attacked by predators. The walrus also has a thick layer of blubber under its skin that protects it from the freezing water. When the temperature drops, the walrus' blood vessels get smaller, helping it maintian its body heat.

FEATURES

- The walrus is known for its large size and pink-reddish brown coloring.
- It is also easily recognized by its large tusks, which it uses to pull itself out of the water onto ice.

FUN FACTS

- The tusks of the walrus have growth rings, just like a tree, and they are highly prized as collectors items.
- The male uses its tusks to establish dominance.
- The walrus uses its whiskers to find food. It then blows a jet stream of water on the food to uncover it or get it to move, so that it can capture and eat it.
- The walrus' main predators are polar bears, killer whales, and humans.
- Native Alaskan people carve beautiful pictures and designs in the harvested tusks of the walrus. This art is called "scrimshaw."

CLASS:	Mammalia (mammals)
ORDER:	Carnivora (meat-eating)
SUBORDER:	Pinnipedia (fin-footed)
FAMILY:	Odobenidae (walruses)
GENUS/SPECIES:	*Odobenus rosmarus*
Size:	8–12 ft (2.4–3.7 m); males larger than females.
Weight:	From 1 to over 2 tons (900–1,800 kg)
Diet:	Snails, crabs, shrimp, worms, and clams
Habitat:	Open waters of the Arctic Ocean near the edge of the polar ice in Northeast Siberia, Northwest Alaska, Greenland, and Ellesmere Island

ALLIGATOR SNAPPING TURTLE

ALLIGATOR SNAPPING TURTLE

CREATED ON DAY 5

DESIGN

The alligator snapping turtle has a fascinating hunting technique. Since this creature eats primarily fish, it spends most of its time in the water. It waits motionless with its mouth open. It then moves its worm-like tongue to entice fish into its mouth. This hunting practice was not part of the original created kind, since all animals were originally vegetarian.

FEATURES

- The alligator snapping turtle is usually brown, black, green, or gray in color with a distinct yellow pattern around its eyes.
- The most distinguishing features of this turtle are the three large ridges that run from the front to the back of its shell.
- The alligator snapping turtle is active both day and night.

FUN FACTS

- This turtle is the largest freshwater turtle in North America; the largest one on record weighed 236 lbs (107 kg).
- Some people have called the alligator snapping turtle the dinosaur of the turtle world.
- They must be handled with extreme care because of their powerful bite.

CLASS:	Reptilia (reptiles)
ORDER:	Testudines (tortoises and turtles)
FAMILY:	Chelydridae (snapping turtles)
GENUS/SPECIES:	*Macrochelys temminckii*
Size:	Average 26 in (60 cm)
Weight:	155–175 lbs (70–79 kg)
Diet:	Primarily fish, but will eat almost anything, including plants
Habitat:	Typically in southeastern freshwater river systems of the United States

DIAMONDBACK TERRAPIN

DIAMONDBACK TERRAPIN

CREATED ON DAY 5

DESIGN

The adult diamondback terrapin nests on sandy borders of coastal salt marshes or in dunes from June to July. Its maximum egg-laying activity occurs at high tide and ensures that the eggs will be laid above the high water level. The female digs holes 4 to 8 in (10–20 cm) deep, depositing between 4 and 15 pinkish white eggs. The eggs hatch in 9 to 15 weeks. Occasionally after hatching, the young may remain in the nest for the first winter, emerging in April and May to head for ocean waters. This nesting instinct was given to this creature by its Creator.

FEATURES

- The diamondback terrapin's shell is ornately patterned, usually in shades of black, brown, or gray, and its body is gray, brown, yellow, or white with dark spots or streaks.
- Its skull has a bony arch, and its upper lip is white.
- The diamondback terrapin gets its name from the diamond-shapes on its shell.

FUN FACTS

- Each terrapin has a unique pattern of black spots and markings on its skin.
- The excess salt that a terrapin consumes in its diet is excreted through special glands near its eyes.
- Mature females can be almost twice the size of mature males.
- This species spends most of its time in the water.

CLASS: Reptilia (reptiles)
ORDER: Testudines (tortoises and turtles)
FAMILY: Emydidae (box and pond turtles)
GENUS/SPECIES: *Malaclemys terrapin*

Size: Male 5 in (13 cm); female 7.5 in (19 cm)
Diet: Crustaceans, mollusks, fish, and insects
Habitat: Coastal swamps of eastern and southern United States

LEATHERBACK SEA TURTLE

LEATHERBACK SEA TURTLE

CREATED ON DAY 5

DESIGN

The leatherback sea turtle has physiological adaptations that the other six species of sea turtles do not possess. These include a dark body color, a thick layer of fat, a high volume-to-surface ratio, and "countercurrent" heat exchangers in its flippers, which allow the warm blood from the heart to warm the cooler blood returning from the veins. All of these features help the leatherback maintain a core body temperature considerably higher than the surrounding water, allowing this species to range farther north and south into colder ocean waters than the other species.

FEATURES

- The leatherback turtle differs from other sea turtles in that its carapace (top shell) is leathery, instead of hard and immovable.
- It is either dark brown or black in color.
- It has seven logitudinal ridges on its carapace.

FUN FACTS

- This is the largest of all living turtles. The largest on record was a male stranded on the west coast of Wales in 1988. He weighed in at a whopping 2,019 lbs (916 kg).
- The leatherback sea turtle is the only marine turtle whose backbone is not attached to the inside of its shell.
- This species is on the federal Endangered Species List. Loss of nesting beaches and poaching of eggs by humans are the prime causes of its decline.

CLASS:	Reptilia (reptiles)
ORDER:	Testudines (tortoises and turtles)
FAMILY:	Dermochelyidae (leatherback turtle)
GENUS/SPECIES:	*Dermochelys coriacea*
Size:	Average 6 ft (1.9 m) to over 9 ft (2.7 m)
Weight:	Average 1,100 lbs (500 kg)
Diet:	Almost exclusively jellyfish
Habitat:	Tropical, sub-tropical, and temperate oceans of the world

LOGGERHEAD SEA TURTLE

LOGGERHEAD SEA TURTLE

CREATED ON DAY 5

DESIGN

The lungs of the loggerhead sea turtle are adapted to permit a rapid exchange of oxygen and to prevent gasses from being trapped during deep dives. The blood of sea turtles can deliver oxygen efficiently to body tissues even at the pressures encountered during diving. During routine activity a loggerhead sea turtle dives for about 4 to 5 minutes and surfaces to breathe for 1 to 3 seconds. Sea turtles can rest or sleep underwater for several hours at a time.

FEATURES

- The loggerhead turtle is known for its large head and horny beak.
- It also has large jaws and powerful muscles.
- Most loggerhead sea turtles have a reddish brown carapace and a pale yellow plastron (bottom shell).

FUN FACTS

- The loggerhead turtle was greatly hunted at one time for its fat, which was used in cosmetics and some medication.
- This is the most abundant sea turtle species in US coastal waters. Most nesting in the US occurs from North Carolina to southwest Florida.
- The temperature of the nest determines whether the eggs will produce males or females. A cooler nest, below 82.5°F (28°C), will produce more males, and a warmer nest, above 85.1°F (29.5°C), will result in more females. If the nest temperature stays in between, there will be a more balanced number of males and females.

CLASS:	Reptilia (reptiles)
ORDER:	Testudines (tortoises and turtles)
FAMILY:	Cheloniidae (sea turtles)
GENUS/SPECIES:	*Caretta caretta gigas* and *C. caretta caretta* (Pacific and Indian loggerheads) and (Atlantic loggerhead)
Size:	Average 3 ft (1 m)
Weight:	About 250 lbs (113 kg)
Diet:	Fish, crustaceans, zooplankton, and invertebrates
Habitat:	Circumglobal in temperate and tropical seas

MARINE IGUANA

MARINE IGUANA

CREATED ON DAY 5

DESIGN

Being a cold-blooded creature, the marine iguana can spend only a limited time in the cold water surrounding the Galapagos Islands to find its food. After a dive the marine iguana will bask in the sun to raise its body temperature. Another interesting feature of this creature is its ability to excrete concentrated salt crystals from its nasal glands to rid itself of excess salt it consumed while eating algae underwater. These designs are part of the Creator's provision for His creation.

FEATURES

- The marine iguana is usually gray to black in color; but on a few islands this creature may vary in color from shades of red to shades of green.
- It also has a blunt snout and slightly compressed tail.

FUN FACTS

- The size of marine iguanas varies from island to island within the Galapagos group.
- It can make a single dive up to 50 ft (15 m) and stay underwater for up to an hour.
- The marine iguana is an herbivore and feeds exclusively on algae.
- It "sneezes" to remove excess salt from its body.
- The marine iguana is threatened by introduced predators (dogs and cats) to the Galapagos.

CLASS:	Reptilia (reptiles)
ORDER:	Squamata (amphisbaenians, lizards, and snakes)
FAMILY:	Iguanidae (iguanas)
GENUS/SPECIES:	*Amblyrhynchus cristatus*
Size:	Male 4.5 ft (1.4 m); female 2 ft (0.6 m)
Weight:	Males weigh up to 3 lbs (1.4 kg)
Diet:	Algae
Habitat:	The Galapagos Islands, 600 miles west of Ecuador, South America

SEA SNAKE

SEA SNAKE

CREATED ON DAY 5

DESIGN

The sea snake is an air-breathing reptile and must come to the surface to breathe. However, it can spend from 30 minutes to two hours diving between breaths. How does it do this? It has one long cylindrical lung that extends almost the entire length of its body. This is very efficient. It is also able to carry out cutaneous respiration. Oxygen diffuses from sea water across the snake's skin into tiny blood vessels and carbon dioxide diffuses out.

FEATURES

- The sea snake has a paddle-shaped tail that helps it move through the water.
- Its nostrils and glands are on the top of its snout to allow it to breathe easier as it swims through the water.

FUN FACTS

- The sea snake has nostril valves that prevent air from entering the lung while it is underwater.
- Sea snakes are confined to tropical waters and all species are venomous. The venom is composed of neurotoxins and myotoxins. Unlike many land snakes, though, sea snakes are not inclined to bite humans.
- Most cases of humans being bitten involve fishermen bitten when sorting through their catch in fish nets.

CLASS:	Reptilia (reptiles)
ORDER:	Squamata (amphisbaenians, lizards, and snakes)
FAMILY:	Hydrophiidae (sea snakes)
GENUS/SPECIES:	About 52 species
Size:	From 20 in (50 cm) to 7 ft (2.1 m)
Diet:	Fish, fish eggs, and eels
Habitat:	Throughout the Pacific and Indian Oceans; some around the coasts of Central and South America

INDEX

Albatross 171
Alligator Snapping Turtle 211
American Lobster 113
Angelfish, French 33
Anhinga 173
Archerfish 15
Arctic Tern 175
Atlantic Puffin 177
Australian Lungfish 17
Balloonfish (see Long-spine Porcupinefish)
Barracuda 19
Beluga Whale 195
Blacktip Reef Shark 89
Blue Mussel (see Common Mussel)
Blue Shark 91
Blue Streak Wrasse (see Cleaner Fish)
Bonnethead Shark 93
Bottlenose Dolphin 197
Box Jellyfish 115
Butterflyfish 21
California Sea Lion 199
Catfish 23
Chambered Nautilus 117
Chiton 119
Clam, Giant 139
Cleaner Fish 25
Cleaner Shrimp 121
Clown Triggerfish 27
Clownfish, Orange 55
Common Limpet 123
Common Murre 179
Common Mussel 125
Common Sand Dollar 127
Conch, Queen 151
Copper Rockfish 29
Coral 129
Cormorant, Double-crested 181
Cowfish, Longhorn 41
Crab
- Ghost 137
- Hermit 143
- Horseshoe 145

Crawdad (see Crayfish)
Crayfish 131
Cuttlefish 133
Diamondback Terrapin 213
Discus Fish 31
Dolphin, Bottlenose 197
Double-crested Cormorant 181
Duck, Mandarin 191
Eel
- Moray 53
- Spotted Garden 75

Emperor Penguin 183
Feather Duster 135
Filefish, Scrawled 67
Firefish, Purple 59
Flamingo 185
French Angelfish 33
Ghost Crab 137
Giant Clam 139
Giant Octopus 141
Glaucous-winged Gull 187
Great Hammerhead Shark 95
Great White Pelican 189
Gull, Glaucous-winged 187
Guppy 35
Harbor Seal 201
Hawkfish, Longnose 43
Hermit Crab 143
Horned Boxfish (see Longhorn Cowfish)
Horseshoe Crab 145
Humphead Wrasse 37
Iguana, Marine 219
Jellyfish, Box 115
Killer Whale 203
Leatherback Sea Turtle 215
Leopard Shark 97
Limpet, Common 123
Lionfish 39
Lobster, American 113
Loggerhead Sea Turtle 217
Longhorn Cowfish 41
Longnose Hawkfish 43
Long-spine Porcupinefish 45
Lookdown 47
Lungfish, Australian 17
Maine Lobster (see American Lobster)